Rap Music

Look for these and other books in the Lucent Overview Series:

Abortion
Acid Rain
Adoption
Advertising
Alcoholism
Animal Rights
Artificial Organs
The Beginning of Writing
The Brain
Cancer
Censorship
Child Abuse
Children's Rights
Cities
The Collapse of the Soviet Union
Cults
Dealing with Death
Death Penalty
Democracy
Drug Abuse
Drugs and Sports
Drug Trafficking
Eating Disorders
Elections
Endangered Species
The End of Apartheid in South Africa
Energy Alternatives
Espionage
Ethnic Violence
Euthanasia
Extraterrestrial Life
Family Violence
Gambling
Gangs
Garbage
Gay Rights
Genetic Engineering
The Greenhouse Effect
Gun Control
Hate Groups
Hazardous Waste

The Holocaust
Homeless Children
Homelessness
Illegal Immigration
Illiteracy
Immigration
Juvenile Crime
Memory
Mental Illness
Militias
Money
Ocean Pollution
Oil Spills
The Olympic Games
Organ Transplants
Ozone
The Palestinian-Israeli Accord
Pesticides
Police Brutality
Population
Poverty
Prisons
Rainforests
The Rebuilding of Bosnia
Recycling
The Reunification of Germany
Schools
Smoking
Space Exploration
Special Effects in the Movies
Sports in America
Suicide
The UFO Challenge
The United Nations
The U.S. Congress
The U.S. Presidency
Vanishing Wetlands
Vietnam
Women's Rights
World Hunger
Zoos

Rap Music

by Jennifer Keeley

Lucent
Books

LUCENT *Overview Series*

Library of Congress Cataloging-in-Publication Data

Keeley, Jennifer, 1974–
  Rap music / by Jennifer Keeley.
     p. cm. — (Lucent overview series)
  Includes bibliographical references (p.   ) and index.
   ISBN 1-56006-504-4 (alk. paper)
   1. Rap (Music)—History and criticism—Juvenile literature. 2. Rap
(Music)—Social aspects—Juvenile literature. [1. Rap (Music)] I. Title.
II. Series.
  ML3531 .K44 2001
  782.421649—dc21

                                                00-013113

Copyright © 2001 by Lucent Books, Inc.
P.O. Box 289011, San Diego, CA 92198-9011
Printed in the U.S.A.

Contents

Introduction

IN THE MID-1970s rap music began to develop in New York City. At the time it was an unknown type of music that existed in one small corner of a great big city. It was played by DJs who traveled to local parks and community centers, stole electric power for their equipment from city lights, and hosted parties at which they refined their techniques. Few, if any, people at these gatherings knew that rap would revolutionize popular music. No one could have guessed the controversy it would cause or the debates it would ignite.

Roughly fifteen years later, people across the United States couldn't stop talking about rap music, specifically, a Florida group named 2 Live Crew. The group's album, *As Nasty as They Wanna Be*, had been labeled something that no other sound recording in U.S. history had—U.S. District Court judge Jose Gonzalez Jr. had declared it "obscene because of its lyrics which were called degrading toward women and overtly offensive to large segments of the population." Since it was now illegal for retailers in Florida to sell the "obscene" album, a record store owner was arrested for doing just that. Hundreds of stores pulled the album from their shelves. Still, other retailers continued to sell *As Nasty as They Wanna Be,* and the record's popularity only increased with the controversy. It had sold nearly 2 million copies when Luther Campbell, one of the members of 2 Live Crew, was arrested for performing songs from the album. As the double-platinum (over 2 million records sold) recording artist was handcuffed and led off to jail, he told *Newsweek,* "That's life in the Americas."[1]

Newspapers, magazines, nightly news broadcasts, and television specials were teeming with people who had an opinion concerning what to do about the Crew. Some wanted to prohibit the sale of songs such as "Dirty Nursery Rhymes" and "Me So Horny." Others cited their existence as evidence of America's moral and artistic decline.

Some defenders of 2 Live Crew pointed to the First Amendment and the need to protect the words of *As Nasty as They Wanna Be* in order to preserve its integrity. "Under our form of freedom of speech," Florida senator Connie

Luther Campbell, member of 2 Live Crew, sits in a Florida courtroom awaiting trial after performing songs from the group's album As Nasty as They Wanna Be.

Mack said at the time, "words are protected. Once we begin selectively defining which words are acceptable, we enter a slippery slope where freedom is compromised."[2] Columnist Christopher Hitchens argued that the lyrics of 2 Live Crew were nothing more than a "foulmouthed attitude toward the gentler sex"[3] and should not even require First Amendment protection in order to exist. In Hitchens's opinion—as well as Campbell's—because the members of 2 Live Crew were African American, racism was behind the comments of those who unfairly targeted them because of their lyrics.[4]

The 2 Live Crew controversy is just the tip of the iceberg. Numerous issues in rap music have led to nationwide debate. In fact, rap music has been a starting point for discussions about a number of important issues in American society. It catalyzed a discussion of violence in popular entertainment, in which rap music was both criticized for violent lyrics and lauded for bringing attention to the violence that plagues some of the poorest communities in the United States. Also, the sexism, racism, and other types of bigotry evident in some rap songs have been thoroughly discussed in the media. Perhaps Tricia Rose phrased it best when she wrote, "Rap music brings together a tangle of some of the most complex social, cultural, and political issues in contemporary American society."[5]

1

The Originality of Reconstructed Music

In the 1970s a new African American and Afro-Caribbean youth culture began to take shape in one of the five boroughs of New York City known as the Bronx. Eventually this youth culture would come to be called hip hop, but at the time, even though it had no name, it could be seen. A new type of graffiti covering the sides of subway cars was the most visible evidence of its existence. Graffiti itself was nothing new; for years individuals had given themselves names or "tags" and written them on subway cars and buildings across the city. However, by the mid-1970s, graffiti had evolved from simple tagging into an art form. Artists no longer merely tagged subway cars, they now painted complex multicolored murals that sometimes covered entire subway trains. This elaborate graffiti was one of the cornerstones of hip hop culture, and as is the case with all of hip hop, it was competitive. Artists claimed territory with their work and constantly tried to outdo each other.

While graffiti artists competed with paint and artistic talent, on dance floors in discos throughout the city, young men and a few women—predominantly Latino and African American—competed through dance. The type of dancing they created became another essential part of hip hop culture—breakdancing. Breakdancing got its name because it started out as a collection of moves that dancers performed during the extended instrumental "breaks" of disco tunes. As it progressed, breakdancing became competitive. Dancers belonged to breaking groups, or "crews," and the crews competed against each other for su-premacy in a given neighborhood. Dance moves such as pop-ping and locking, the backspin, the head spin, the moonwalk, the robot, the worm, and many more all came to be associated with breakdancing. Its practitioners—some of hip hop's earliest and most loyal adherents—were called b-boys (and b-girls), which was short for "break" boy.

At first, b-boys and b-girls contented themselves with the musical breaks of songs played at local clubs, but all that changed as a third aspect of hip hop culture began to develop—rap music. Rap represented an entirely new way of thinking about sound. The early rap "disc jockeys" (DJs) did not play traditional instruments, but instead cut back and forth between records playing on two different turntables. In other words, they used these records, which had already

Breakdancing became an essential part of early hip-hop culture.

been recorded, to create new music. Rap artists also did not sing, but instead rhymed half-spoken, half-sung lyrics over their music. Since it was so different from all other types of popular music, rap faced many challenges. Some people questioned whether it could even be considered music because they did not believe it was original or had a traditional melody. Meanwhile, the fact that rap employed a new way of creating music ignited—and continues to ignite—social and legal debates over its originality and ownership. Today rap music and the way it is created are fairly commonplace in the music industry, but at the time of its development, its biggest problem was the fact that it lacked precedent in mainstream culture.

The evolution of rap

In order to comprehend the problems rap music faced because of its originality, it is first necessary to understand what rap music is and how it came into being. Tricia Rose provides a useful definition in her book, *Black Noise: Rap Music and Black Culture in Contemporary America* when she states that rap "is a form of rhymed storytelling accompanied by highly rhythmic, electronically based music."[6] This "highly rhythmic, electronically based music" of which she speaks is typically called hip hop music. It can be difficult to understand the difference between the terms rap music and hip hop music because they are sometimes used interchangeably. Music critic Nelson George, however, makes a distinction when he writes,

> A rap record is a hip hop record. A hip hop record is not necessarily a rap record. . . . Rap records are dominated by the tone and/or words of the rapper, while the music . . . can be in balance with the rapper's voice or may highlight it. However, if the music overwhelms the words it's probably not a rap record but a hip hop record.[7]

In other words, rap is a type of hip hop music in which the spoken/sung vocals are the focus of the song.

The first part of rap to develop was its musical foundation. This began in the South Bronx in the mid-1970s with a very important group of DJs (rap would remain an East Coast phenomenon for roughly a decade). As was the case with the

Afrika Bambaataa (left), one of the Bronx DJs whose performances influenced the development of rap music.

rest of hip hop culture, these DJs were competitive. They claimed territories by building up loyal followings and holding DJ battles.

In the Bronx there were four major DJs, each with his own territory: Kool Herc (Clive Campbell), Grandmaster Flash (Joseph Saddler), Afrika Bambaataa (Afrika Bambaataa Aasim), and DJ Breakout. While these DJs did play in local clubs, they also took their sound systems and extensive record collections to different parks and school yards to provide the music for outdoor, community gatherings. The mobile DJs would open up the bases of streetlights and use the power boxes inside to provide the power they needed for their electrical equipment. Then they would get the party going by playing or "spinning" records while people gathered, listened, rhymed over the beat, wrote graffiti, or breakdanced.

However, they were not simply playing records, they were using them to create a new type of music. It was Kool Herc (Clive Campbell) who started it all when he created break spinning. He realized that the part of the song the b-boys and b-girls really loved to dance to was the break beat—the portion without vocals or other instruments where the drummer and the bass guitarist take their solos. Therefore, instead of offering audiences songs in their entirety, Herc would buy two copies of each song and play only the break beat. With it queued up on two turntables, Herc would cut back and forth, prolonging the break beat until it became a song in and of itself.

Herc's break spinning became a building block of hip hop music. The other Bronx DJs built upon his work in the mid to late seventies and founded some of the practices that today are closely identified with hip hop and rap music. A technique called "scratching," or manually moving the needle back and forth on one record to create a rhythm that is played along with or against the rhythm of a second record, was created by a thirteen-year-old named Grand Wizard Theodore. However, it was Grandmaster Flash who perfected it and

Grandmaster Flash is credited with inventing or perfecting numerous techniques and innovations associated with rap music.

made it popular. Flash is also credited with numerous other innovations including backspinning—manually spinning the record backward to repeat a portion of a song—and using a drum machine to play in time with the rhythm of a given record, thereby enhancing the beat.

All of these technical achievements improved the music, but rap is considered rap because of its vocals. These vocals came about as DJs became popular and drew larger followings. Tricia Rose explains that, "DJ performance attracted large excited crowds, but it also began to draw the crowd's attention away from dancing and toward watching the DJ perform. It is at this point that rappers were added to the DJs' shows to redirect the crowd's attention."[8] As DJs began to add lyricists—called MCs, short for master of ceremonies—these artists directed the audience's attention by rhyming over the DJs' music, usually boasting and telling stories to the crowd. Slowly, MCs developed distinct styles of rhyming, dressing, and even dancing. Soon they had followings of their own, and eventually they stole the spotlight from the DJs. MCs' rhymes became as important as the music and sometimes even more so, and as they did, rap music was born.

That's not music, or is it?

Throughout the latter part of the 1970s, rap gained in popularity in New York City. This increased popularity led to some small, independent record labels taking a risk and signing artists to record rap songs. One of these early rap singles, the Sugar Hill Gang's "Rapper's Delight," was released in October of 1979 and is credited with introducing the world to rap music. When it rose to number four on the *Billboard* R&B chart, this popularity suggested that people across the country—not just those in New York City—were interested in the new music. In fact, this song became so closely associated with the new music that MCs came to be called "rappers" instead.

However, the rap artists were introducing people to a music that lacked precedent, which also caused problems. It is important to understand that until the emergence of hip hop and rap, the majority of popular music—for exam-

ple, rock and roll—was created by trained musicians who wrote, played, and sang original music. Rap, on the other hand, typically consisted of drumbeats from a machine, pieces called "samples" from previously recorded material, scratching, and spoken/sung lyrics that had no melody in the way previous forms of music had. The fact that rap was something entirely new meant that people reacted to it in different ways.

Advocates of rap argued, in the words of Lynn Norment, that "in the midst of urban decay and hopelessness, this creative expression [rap] was born of frustration with social ills."[9] They asserted that its rhymed storytelling was a form of street poetry, that rap was a music expressing the concerns of inner-city African Americans, concerns that typically went unnoticed in the United States.

Still, not everyone thought so highly of rap music. "Loud, pounding rhythm with shouted lyrics and no melody do not constitute music,"[10] declared an angry letter to the editor that appeared in the *New York Times*. This comment is typical of

Members of the Sugar Hill Gang perform "Rapper's Delight," a song often credited with introducing the world to rap music.

many that were made in the early days of rap music. To back up their claims that rap was not music, some people pointed to the fact that rap producers were not formally trained musicians, rap artists did not play traditional instruments, and rap lyrics had no melody. Ian Steaman recalled the hostility that rap faced in its early days in a 1992 article for *Billboard:*

> When hip-hop began its development some 15 years ago in New York, it was dismissed as a passing fad by critics. Simple chanting over beats wasn't music, they said; rap was merely the crude utterances of ghetto hoodlums who didn't have the musical training and sophistication to create "real" music.[11]

This belief that rap was not real music was only further reinforced at the time by the difficulty people had finding it on the radio. There were a few college stations where students created rap shows. However, even in New York City where rap began, in 1980 there was only one regularly scheduled rap-format broadcast—Mr. Magic's Rap Attack—and this aired from 2 A.M. to 5 A.M. on New Jersey's WHBI. It would be another couple of years before there were more rap broadcasts, and, before these broadcasts garnered better time slots.

Does sampling create an original?

While some people debated whether or not rap was music, others conceded its musicality but questioned its originality. This occurred because rap was not merely a new music, but also a new way of making music. Since the days of DJ Kool Herc, artists created rap through sampling. Live DJs used records, turntables, quick hands, and impeccable timing to create their sound. When it came time to record rap songs for records, some rappers used their turntables, while others chose to rap over bands that recreated the sound of turntable sampling by playing break beats the way a DJ would have spun them—for example the Sugar Hill Gang in "Rapper's Delight." However, as technology advanced, artists traded in their turntables and live bands and turned to "samplers" to create rap music.

Samplers are computers that can record and digitize—convert into a form that the computer understands—any sound. Once a sound is recorded, it can be manipulated. A person using a sampler can change the sound's key, tone, pitch, quality, and just about everything else, then play it back. When more than one sound is recorded, the sampler can play back sounds in any sequence and even loop them—play and replay a sequence of sounds endlessly.

The first computer that could be used for sampling appeared in the late seventies, and by the early eighties the first samplers designed specifically for sampling were available. Before the advent of rap music, sampling was primarily used as a shortcut in the recording process. For example, if a song needed a trumpet, a producer could use a sampler to record one from an existing song and then manipulate it to fit the new song being recorded. This saved a great deal of time and money in the recording process since extra musicians did not have to be hired and paid.

However, rap music used the sampler in an entirely new way. Whereas other music used sampling to fill holes in the

Since the days of DJ Kool Herc (pictured), rap artists have employed a musical technique known as sampling.

production process, rap DJs used samples from numerous songs to construct a whole new song. Also, as Tricia Rose points out, "Prior to rap, the most desirable use of a sample was to mask the sample and its origin; to bury its identity. Rap producers . . . inverted this logic, using [well-known] samples as a point of reference."[12]

Of course, these samples had to be created in order for DJs, rap artists, and producers to use them. Therefore, as rap itself became more well-known, some people asserted that it was not original because they believed it simply recycled the work of other artists. One artist who questioned the originality of rap was Mtume, a famous producer-songwriter who penned tunes such as "The Closer I Get to You" and "I Never Knew Love Like This Before." In his book, *Hip Hop America,* Nelson George recalled Mtume's criticisms of rap music as he expressed them on a 1988 radio show:

> Mtume spent much of this particular Sunday morning [show] blasting hip hop record production for its slavish reliance on record sampling. He charged that "this is the first generation of African Americans not to be extending the range of the music." To further illustrate his disdain, Mtume made a bold analogy: sampling James Brown's drum beats in a hip hop album was like [an author] sticking chapters from James Baldwin [books] in [their] books and claiming the words as [their own].[13]

Rap's defenders responded to allegations such as these by saying that artists sampled from songs to create something entirely new. Critic Gene Santoro called hip hop a "startling thing, a new way to imagine sound." He then spoke about the originality of this reconstructed music, saying, "Looping, defacing and recontextualizing isolated snippets ("samples") from old records . . . [artists mold] shredded musical history [samples from numerous songs] into new shapes [songs] within a single tune behind a singsong, usually macho, deep-voiced, street-style poetry."[14]

The first law of sampling

Debates between critics over the musical validity of rap soon took a backseat to legal issues raised by the new ways that rap artists created music. Since sampling involves the reformulation and rerecording of music that is copyrighted

For his song "I'll Be Missing You," Puff Daddy needed permission from Sting to use samples from "Every Breath You Take."

(that is, "owned" by a musician or music company), the sampled music legally belongs to that musician or company. It cannot be reproduced without coming to some sort of legal agreement with that musician or company. For instance, when Puff Daddy sampled Sting's "Every Breath You Take" to make "I'll Be Missing You," he had to come to an agreement with Sting to sample the song or risk being sued for using Sting's music without permission.

In the early days of rap music this was a fairly easy issue to resolve, partly because at the time the genre of rap did not have many listeners or buyers. Therefore, the use of samples either went unnoticed or no one pursued the issue in court since they would only receive a share of the profits, and these were small—in most cases not enough to cover the legal costs of obtaining royalties (money for letting another artist use their work). However, a few early rap songs were popular, and with popularity came profits, and with profits came accusations of theft and legal battles over copyrighted music.

Not surprisingly, the first rap song to turn a substantial profit faced a legal challenge about sampling. In making "Rapper's Delight," the Sugar Hill Gang sampled a disco hit by Chic called "Good Times." Bernard Edwards and Nile Rodgers, who wrote "Good Times" and owned the song, later sued the owner of Sugar Hill Records and received full songwriting credit and a share of the royalties for "Rapper's Delight." The case set a legal precedent, that record companies would have to come to an agreement with the owner of a sample when it was heavily used. Obtaining this agreement is known as sample clearing.

More rules, and more creativity

After the "Rapper's Delight" decision, artists were driven by creativity as well as financial considerations to begin sampling small, isolated bits of songs, because at the time this could be done without clearance. In the late eighties and early nineties some of rap's groundbreaking albums were recorded in this way. Albums such as Public Enemy's *It Takes a Nation of Millions to Hold Us Back*, De La Soul's *3 Feet High and Rising*, and N.W.A.'s *Straight Outta Compton* are, in the words of critic Suzanne McElfresh, "constructed from multiple samples and densely layered, a song from any one of these albums plays like a mini-archive of pop music."[15]

These albums were landmarks in the creative art of sampling because producers were able to assemble innumerable small bits from songs from all different genres and time periods. They then artfully pieced these samples together to create a seamless original sound. Albums such as *It Takes a Nation of Millions* and *3 Feet High and Rising* are still considered, by music critics such as McElfresh and Nelson George, to be some of the most important hip hop albums to date because of the complexity of the music.

However, these same critics point out that such albums would be too expensive to make today. This is due, in part, to a change in the legal landscape that resulted from two lawsuits in the early 1990s. The first was a lawsuit brought against De La Soul for their album *3 Feet High and Rising*. A 1960s rock group called the Turtles sued the rappers because they used a very small snippet from a Turtles' song. In the end, the case was settled out of court. The Turtles received a hefty sum and as a result record companies started to become leery of using even small pieces of songs without clearance.

The Turtles' victory was just the beginning. Soon after, Gilbert O'Sullivan sued rapper Biz Markie for the unauthorized use of a sample from his 1972 hit "Alone Again (Naturally)" on Markie's 1992 *I Need a Haircut* album. The future of sampling—as well as rap music—was changed forever when a federal court judge ruled in O'Sullivan's favor. Now

The future of rap music and sampling was forever changed after Biz Markie (center) was sued for illegally using samples.

even small samples had to be paid for and therefore the more small samples a song had, the more expensive it was to produce.

However, the most disturbing part of this case for the rap music industry was the fact that O'Sullivan was able to hold the record company hostage. He made them recall *I Need a Haircut* until the song in question was removed. Previously, record companies had allowed questionable samples—samples where it was legally unclear whether or not they had to pay the owner—to remain in songs. After the Markie-O'Sullivan decision they could no longer "gamble" in this way because it might ultimately be too expensive. In other words, record companies could not release songs with small samples and pay the copyright holders in the event they came forward. If the companies did not pay up front, they risked losing a great deal of money if they would have to recall the album.

Around the time the decision was handed down, lawyer Andy Tavel discussed its immediate effects and speculated about the future. "People who have had one or two words sampled . . . are now coming out of the woodwork and saying, 'Look at this case, pay me,'" Tavel said. "Now, record companies are going to insist that every sample be cleared. It's greatly going to increase cost."[16] For the most part, Tavel's predictions were correct. Nine months later, Havelock Nelson reported in *Billboard* magazine that the Markie-O'Sullivan decision had "prompted more than a few major labels to initiate 'ultrasafe' sample-clearing procedures."[17] Nelson added that this had resulted in delays of a number of albums and a significant increase in production expenses.

In response to these two court decisions, rap artists once again came up with new ways to create music. At present, some artists and producers meet legal standards by sampling heavily from a limited number of songs and reaching agreements with the owners up front. Others have become more creative and clever in sampling, utilizing extremely small and obscure portions of sound to circumvent existing laws. While this does make it difficult to reference other songs through sampling, it has led to increased creativity and a recent trend toward original compositions. This has some rap artists believing rap is moving in a whole new creative direction. One such artist is Rza, the producing star of the rap group Wu-Tang Clan, who suggests that rap and hip hop artists "will be the songwriters of the future."[18]

Whatever the future of rap music might be, its past and present have been filled with obstacles because it began as an entirely new way of thinking about music. While some of the debates that encircled the genre in its infancy have been settled, others such as legal debates over sampling will undoubtedly remain in the future. These debates, however, will most likely inspire new creativity and the continuing evolution of rap.

2

Selling Records or Selling Out?

IN THE EARLY years of its development, rap's creators, performers, and listeners were predominantly African American. As a result, when a larger audience was introduced to rap in the late seventies, it was labeled a black form of music. Such categorization was not unusual. Throughout the history of popular music in the United States, music has been classified by the race of its creators and performers. Musical forms such as the blues, jazz, rhythm and blues (R&B), rap, and hip hop have all been labeled "black" at some time in their histories.

This racial separation of music also affected radio play. As radio stations formed and began playing popular music, "white" and "black" stations developed. "White" stations played popular songs by white performers and "black" stations played those by African American performers. This meant that whether a song was considered to be white or black greatly affected the radio audience it reached. For a variety of reasons—but mainly because there are many more white people in the United States than black—white stations tended to have much larger audiences. Since the audience a song reaches contributes in large part to its popularity and record sales, African American musicians who performed music that appealed to white audiences were more commercially successful than those who did not.

Rap's unique situation

Since the advent of rock and roll in the 1950s, white and black listeners have listened to a great deal of the same music and black artists sometimes were accepted into the mainstream, white pop charts. By the 1970s many African American R&B artists enjoyed "crossover" success in the pop charts because of the dominance of disco, a music that borrowed heavily from rhythm and blues. However, in the late seventies and early eighties a nationwide backlash against disco music created an obvious separation between the music that white listeners and black listeners enjoyed, the likes of which had not been seen in nearly thirty years. "The death of disco had an important effect on the pop scene," Steve Greenberg writes, "especially in radio, where [people] were shying away from black records of any kind in an effort to stay as far from the 'disco' tag as possible."[19] Rap came onto the music scene just as disco faded from the charts. As a result, rap evolved in a very unique atmosphere. In *The Vibe History of Hip Hop*, Greenberg explains the separation of black and white music in the period in which rap developed:

> While in a typical week in the first half of 1979 nearly 50 percent of the records on *Billboard*'s pop singles chart could also be found on the R & B chart, by the first half of 1980 that number had dropped to 21 percent, and by the end of 1982 the crossover percentage was at a rock-era low of 17 percent. In the extreme, October 1982 saw a three-week period during which not one record by an African-American could be found in the Top 20 on *Billboard*'s pop singles or albums charts.[20]

While some rap songs did make it into the Top 40 in the early eighties, the chances of doing so were slim because of the continuing stigma against R&B-based dance music. With little possibility of reaching a mass, predominantly white audience, the record labels that signed rap artists did not worry about producing music that would appeal to this demographic. Instead, some allowed their artists to make music for music's sake. Likewise, the early artists who developed rap music in the streets and clubs of New York did not expect to earn a great deal of money. In fact, as Nelson George points out, "Money was not the goal. None of the three original DJs—Herc, Flash, Bambaataa—expected anything from the

In the early days of rap, artists like Grandmaster Flash focused more on creating music than on record sales.

music but local fame, respect in the neighborhood."[21] In other words, since there was little hope of reaching a mass audience in the early days of rap, there was little pressure on artists to create songs that would have commercial appeal in mainstream America; the emphasis was on musicality and creativity instead of selling records.

However, it was only a matter of time until the wall between white and black music came down. Predominantly young, white listeners were drawn to the unique sounds they did not hear on the stale, unchanging pop charts. Soon significant numbers of listeners outside the African American community began to take notice of rap, and by the mid-eighties rap artists were enjoying limited crossover success. Whereas some people saw rap's newfound popularity in mainstream America as an opportunity to spread the unique—often political—messages of rap songs to new people and places, it angered some hip hop purists. They wondered what would happen when rap artists and record labels saw the financial benefits of marketing rap to the masses and feared that record companies and artists would be enticed to "sell out," or simplify their music and eliminate any controversial views or political messages in an effort to sell records.

Pop rap

Rap artists such as M.C. Hammer, Will Smith, Young MC, and Puff Daddy created a type of rap music that appealed to mainstream America and sold quite a few albums in the process. Every one of these artists has had a song enjoy crossover success on the pop charts. In order to do so, they had to draw millions of new listeners to rap music.

Will Smith was one of many artists whose rap music appealed to mainstream America.

Because of his commercial success, M.C. Hammer has been labeled a sellout by other rappers.

However, these same artists have also been accused of selling out because their music is seen as feel-good music that emphasizes danceability over rhyme skills. In other words, they are criticized for creating "bubblegum rap records" instead of complex music—a criticism that is, incidentally, leveled against a great deal of pop music of all genres.

In 1990 Jay Cocks discussed how M.C. Hammer dealt with charges of selling out. "Hammer has been called out by the rap press ('cheesy, pop-oriented production') and torched by fellow rappers from Digital Underground to M.C. Serch and 3rd Bass. . . . [He] handles such criticism with equanimity. 'Rather than cross over [into the pop market], let's say that I expanded,' [Hammer] suggests. 'My music caught on because the people are ready for it.'"[22]

There are also rap artists who applaud the success of pop rap acts such as M.C. Hammer's. "You're supposed to sell out!" Chuck D of Public Enemy told *Rolling Stone* as he admired Hammer's pop success. "If you got fifteen tapes on the shelf, your mission is to sell. So I can't get mad at Hammer for doing what he's got to do."[23]

In his 1990 article in *Ebony*, Charles Whitaker pointed out that relatively few message-oriented rappers took issue with those who produced "innocuous party rap" and quoted party pop-rapper Marvin Young (Young MC) on the matter. "It's about new attitudes and ideas being expressed," said Young, "and that's good for rap because it gets more people into the music and expands the record-buying base for everybody."[24] Some artists, critics, and rap music executives believe it is precisely this expanded record-buying base that has sustained rap music and kept it from being just a short-lived fad.

Politics and popularity

Rap's longevity is especially important to those who see it as a tool for social and political change. The first group to successfully use rap as a vehicle for a social and political message was Grandmaster Flash and the Furious Five. In 1982 this group was known for their carefree party music, but they changed the course of rap when they released a song called "The Message." Steve Greenberg explains the effect this song had on the entire genre of rap:

> In 1982's "The Message," the Furious Five proved that rap could be more than just a novelty. Its intensely frank view of ghetto life marked a turning point for hip hop, which from then on would regularly express the desperation and rage felt in the black community. . . . In the record's wake, hip hop MCs could no longer duck the idea of dealing seriously with issues facing their community.[25]

Public Enemy's pro-black political message was popular among both black and white audiences.

"The Message" drew the attention of many music critics and made it to number four on the R&B charts. Its commercial success paved the way for political expression in rap, a practice that would be taken to a whole new level five years later with Public Enemy.

Public Enemy was an overtly political group that came onto the rap scene in the late eighties. Still today they are

seen, in the words of Nelson George, as "the exemplars of aggressive, political music."[26] Their music expressed black nationalist ideologies and discussed racism in ways that no other music had. The group itself was involved in political issues such as getting recognition of the Martin Luther King Jr. holiday in Arizona (among other things, they wrote a song titled "By the Time I Get to Arizona" to bring national attention to the issue).

Yet, even though Public Enemy had a pro-black message, they attracted a large following of young white people. "It was very strange to see white guys get into Public Enemy's music, when Public Enemy, to a great extent, was talking against white guys,"[27] journalist Harry Allen recalled. Critics who had feared that the popularity of rap would lead artists to tone down their politics were mystified by white youth's interest in Public Enemy and what it meant for rap music and society. They wondered what drew young white people to songs such as "Fight the Power," which called white historical and cultural figures racists and contained pro-black messages such as "I'm Black and I'm Proud."[28] The question was, were these listeners understanding the message? David Samuels did not think so and argued that Public Enemy's success had more to do with "a highly charged theater of race in which [white] listeners became guilty eavesdroppers on the . . . private conversation of the inner city,"[29] than white listeners actually hearing the group's political message.

As for Public Enemy's thoughts on the matter, "[Chuck D's] vision was—and still is—that out of this music will come new life," Harry Allen told VH1. "Seeds will be planted that will grow, the effects of which we will only see down the road."[30] Chuck D is not the only person who believes that some rap songs successfully pass on a social or political message to young people, and the more people—black or white—that listen to a song, the greater the possibility someone will hear its political message. Ian Steaman writes that political rap is a "method of conveying political statement and promoting a world view that [isn't] reflected in the mainstream media"[31] and other critics agree. These critics admit that there may be plenty of rap listeners who do

Made popular by groups like N.W.A., gangsta rap uses profanity and obscene lyrics to describe life in the urban ghetto.

not understand its political significance, but that this does not mean that it has no impact on those who do.

The mass appeal of gangsta rap

In the early nineties it became apparent through Sound-Scan statistics that white, predominantly suburban, male teens were purchasing a great deal of rap called gangsta, hardcore, or reality rap. Gangsta rap is a type of rap that originated on the West Coast in the late eighties and was made famous by artists such as Ice-T and N.W.A. Its songs typically use a great deal of profanity to depict life in some of the poorest, most downtrodden communities; celebrate violence, drugs, and gang life; and discuss issues such as loyalty to male friends and the evil women do.

Since life in an urban ghetto seemed very different from the lifestyle of suburban, white males, the popularity of

Some critics claim that white, suburban males listen to gangsta rap because it reinforces negative stereotypes about African Americans.

gangsta rap in these areas became a topic of debate. "If you're a suburban white kid and you want to find out what life is like for a black city teenager, you buy a record by N.W.A.," famed producer Hank Shocklee said when asked about the mass appeal of gangsta rap. "It's like going to an amusement park and getting on a roller coaster ride—records are safe, they're controlled fear, and you always have the choice of turning it off."[32]

Some critics believed that the desire of artists and record companies to market to young, white suburbanites caused problems. They argued that these young people were attracted to gangsta rap because some songs reinforced the negative stereotypes they had about African Americans and worried that some artists were selling out, essentially by giving paying fans what they wanted—negative images of African Americans.

Critic Jay Cocks addressed this in his review of the gangsta rap group N.W.A.'s album *Efil4zaggin*. Cocks told his readers that N.W.A. started "an entire open season for negative stereotyping" and accused the group of making the stereotype of African American males as murderous thugs come to life to entertain white audiences. Cocks concluded that some rap songs were like mini horror movies and "Rappers like N.W.A. and Public Enemy want to scare the living hell out of white America—and sell it a whole mess of records—by making its worst racial nightmares come true."[33] Critics such as Cocks believed that mainstream interest in gangsta rap music led to a situation in which African American gangsta rappers who want to appeal to this mass audience reinforce negative stereotypes of African Americans in order to sell records.

Thus, rap has been criticized at every step for its popularity with mainstream audiences, and its complex and controversial relationship with its mainstream fans is still a topic of discussion today. However, whether or not critics believe that rap's move into the mainstream is an asset or a detriment, they all admit that there is no going back. While they continue to scrutinize the complex reasons that mass audiences enjoy rap music, rap songs remain squarely at the top of the pop charts. Rap's popularity is now commonplace in history, and there is no doubt that listeners of all types will continue to enjoy rap songs in years to come.

3

Violent Lyrics, Violent Lifestyle

A few individual songs are seen as precursors to gangsta rap, but its official beginning is usually cited as the late 1980s when Ice-T (Tracy Marrow) and groups such as N.W.A. exploded onto the music scene. This new form of rap came from the West Coast and specifically Los Angeles (previously rap music had been an East Coast phenomenon). It sounded completely different musically than anything that had preceded it and it also had very different lyrics that celebrated violence, crack cocaine, and male sexual prowess, among other things. These gritty and violent lyrics set off a debate that continues today. While there were many slight and subtle variations, for the most part there were two sides to this controversy. Essentially, debate boiled down to a question of which came first, violent lyrics or increased violence in the inner cities around the United States.

Rap-related violence

Popular music has always had an uneasy relationship with violence. From fifties rock and roll to present-day rap concerts, audience members have been involved in brawls, rapes, stabbings, shootings, and numerous other criminal activities while listening to their favorite groups. However, for a variety of reasons, mainstream Americans came to associate rap, more than other types of popular music, with violence.

Unfortunately, this was in part because there was actual violence at some rap concerts. Even one of the first big rap tours, Run-DMC's "Raising Hell" tour, had to deal with unruly fans. *Time* magazine described an incident that occurred on Run-DMC's Long Beach, California tour stop where "more than 300 members of black and Hispanic street gangs swarmed through the crowd, attacking everyone around them."[34] Violence at concerts was nothing new. Such incidents

Ice-T was one of the first gangsta rappers to explode on the music scene.

Members of Run-DMC hold a press conference after their Long Beach concert ended in violence.

occurred at rock and roll, heavy metal, and even country music concerts. However, violence at rap concerts was seen by some to be linked to rap music in a way that violence at rock concerts was not linked to rock music. Adding that the Long Beach incident was the fourth incident of violence on the tour, *Time* magazine quoted Public Safety Commissioner John Norton as saying, "There is absolutely no doubt in my mind that rap music spurs violence."[35]

Some critics contend that it was actually the media's biased coverage of violence at rap events that cemented a link between rap and violence in the minds of many Americans. According to Tricia Rose, this coverage has always had more to do with white America's fear of, and desire to control, black youth than it has to do with actual violence that occurs. She argues that the real issue is that "the presence of a predominantly black audience in a 15,000 capacity arena, communicating with major black cultural icons whose music, lyrics, and attitude illuminate and affirm black fears and grievances, provokes a fear of . . . black rage."[36]

Rose further states that the result of this fear is biased media coverage that focuses on concert violence, falsely equates it with rap music, and spawns catchphrases such as "rap-related violence" that become self-fulfilling prophecies. For example, a reporter who goes to a rap concert looking for rap-related violence will probably be able to find some violent incident about which to write. On the other hand, if a reporter goes to a rock concert to see the band and violence occurs, it will most likely be written off as a small incident unassociated with the music.

Violent lyrics cause violence

Whether the result of actual concert violence or a media creation, rap was linked to violence in the minds of many Americans long before gangsta rap became part of the pop music picture. This notion was only further reinforced as the lyrics of some songs became increasingly violent with the advent of gangsta rap.

Some people believed that the violent lyrics of this new music led to increased violence in the United States. While they were united in this belief, these social critics did not agree on the extent that rap lyrics influenced violence. Some contended that these lyrics promoted violence by making it seem a prerequisite for manhood. Others asserted that the violent actions of the artists themselves, whom children consider role models, encouraged young people to be violent. Finally, there were some critics who maintained that gangsta rap music actually caused violence by suggesting scenarios to its listeners or acting as a "triggering" device for violent acts.

In a 1995 issue of *Newsweek*, Michael Marriott expressed his concerns that young people were starting to believe in what he saw as a violent philosophy of gangsta rap. "Gangster rappers who extol the virtues of bullets, bitches and 40-ounce beers, of 'getting paid' and pocketing 'mad loot,' have been idolized as urban heroes," he wrote. "The ghetto-centric lifestyles projected in their lyrics and videos, and their 'hard,' take-no-prisoners ethos [philosophy], have become standards for millions of swaggering, pants-sagging Americans, both black and white."[37]

Man-on-the-street interviews indicated that everyday people had similar concerns about the violence of rap music and its effect on young people. A member of the administration at Jersey City State College told reporters that "Gangsta rap tends to deliver violent messages . . . [that] suggest to the younger generation that to get respect or to be a 'man,' one should be tough, make money 'by any means necessary,' carry a gun, and be prepared to use it."[38] This is a frequent criticism of gangsta rap music—that it makes it seem as though a male

N.W.A. (pictured) and other gangsta rappers have been accused of glamorizing violence through their music.

must be violent to be a man. Because many young boys listen to rap songs, people worry that some of them may come to believe violence is a part of manhood.

Since rap artists are role models for some young people, these critics argue that matters are only made worse when the rap artists themselves commit violent acts, and some of the most prominent gangsta rap artists have done exactly that. In an article titled "Shootin' up the Charts," Richard Lacayo recounts a three-week period in 1993 when three rap artists were charged with crimes: Tupac Shakur was charged in the shooting of two off-duty police officers; Calvin Broadus (Snoop Dogg) was charged as an accomplice to murder; and Public Enemy's Flavor Flav was arrested for attempted murder.

In 1993 popular gangsta rappers Snoop Doggy Dogg (left) and Tupac Shakur (right) were charged with violent crimes.

Everton Bailey, president of the New York men's group Brothers United to Save Our Youth, suggests that there might be a connection between gangsta rappers resorting to gun violence to solve their problems and the gun use of children. He says, "Kids look up to rap artists as role models, and because of the behavior of a lot of [rap artists], a lot of kids are taking guns to schools and shooting fellow students and teachers."[39] Nathan McCall, *Washington Post* reporter and author, also sees a correlation between lyrical violence and actual violence. He told *Newsweek,* "There are obviously some correlations between the constant negative violent messages that are being put out in rap and the violence that exists out there in the real world."[40]

One of the most infamous incidents in rap music history came about, at least in part, because of this belief that violent lyrics promote violence. The FBI's assistant director of public affairs, Milt Ahlerich, sent a letter to N.W.A.'s record label, Priority Records, regarding the group's debut album, *Straight Outta Compton*, which contained the song, "F___ Tha Police." The letter stated that N.W.A.'s music "encourages violence against and disrespect for the law enforcement official." Ahlerich's letter continued:

> Advocating violence and assault is wrong. . . . Violence, a major problem in our country, reached an unprecedented level in 1988. Seventy-eight law enforcement officials were feloniously slain in the line of duty during 1988, four more than 1987. . . . Recordings such as these are both discouraging and degrading to the brave, dedicated officers. . . .
>
> Music plays a significant role in society, and I wanted you to be aware of the FBI's position relative to this song and its message.[41]

While Ahlerich may have implied that N.W.A.'s music could lead to actual violence, few people ever directly connect a real-life violent act to a rap song. However, there have been instances where this has occurred. In a column for *Newsweek*, George Will argued that young men who were tried for the gang rape of a Central Park jogger had gotten the idea from a 2 Live Crew song. "Where can you get the idea that sexual violence against women is fun?" he asked. "From a music store, through

Walkman earphones, from boom boxes blaring forth the rap lyrics of 2 Live Crew."[42]

Can lyrics "trigger" violence?

The theory that violent rap lyrics cause real violence was even tested in a court of law. In June 1993, nineteen-year-old Ronald Ray Howard was convicted of shooting a Texas police officer and faced the possibility of being sentenced to death for his actions. At the sentencing hearing, Howard's attorney, Allen Tanner, made the argument that the gangsta rap music his client was listening to at the time the police officer pulled him over had contributed to the shooting. Howard was allegedly listening to Tupac's *2Pacalypse Now* and a tape by Ganksta N.I.P., a local rap artist.

Some critics argue that gangsta rap's antipolice lyrics incite violence against police officers.

[Tanner argued that listening to gangsta rap with antipolice lyrics impacted his client's decision to shoot the officer.] He tried to show that listening to the music had placed Howard in an antipolice mind-set, making it all the easier for him to pull the trigger when confronted with a police officer. To support this theory that music could "trigger" violent actions, Tanner put Howard's ex-girlfriend on the stand. She testified, "Howard would listen to rap music and pretend to shoot a gun when the songs talked about killing police."[43] Tanner also called an expert witness, Joe Steussy, Ph.D., director of the music division at the University of Texas at San Antonio. Steussy testified, "If someone already had an antipolice mind-set, music containing similar sentiments would reinforce those feelings. If such an individual were stopped by a police officer while driving a stolen car . . . [the] music can become a 'triggering device' for actions like the murder."[44] While Tanner, Steussy, Howard, and others—

including the slain police officer's wife who went on to file a civil suit against Shakur for his lyrics—believed in this "trigger" theory, prosecutor Bobby Bell called it "the devil-made-me-do-it defense."[45] The jury agreed with Bell and dismissed this argument, sentencing Howard to death.

Gangsta rap vs. law enforcement

"They say we're a bad influence; we promote violence and everything else," N.W.A.'s Eric Wright (Eazy-E) told reporters in 1989 in response to criticism about *Straight Outta Compton*. "Number one is we don't. It's just like they try to hide what's going on and we tell it like it is."[46] This, then, is the other side of the violent lyrics debate—rappers argued that they were only documenting the reality of their urban environment and that reality was violent long before their songs came into being. In other words, they maintained that it was not violent lyrics that caused violence, but violence that caused them to write violent lyrics.

Gangsta rap deals with some of the harsh realities of living in an urban ghetto or other economically depressed neighborhood. Gangsta rappers sing about the pervasiveness of drugs, especially crack cocaine, and the problems associated

Drugs and the problems associated with them are topics covered in gangsta rap.

with the drug trade. Gang warfare, murder, the death of friends and loved ones, and run-ins with law enforcement are just a few of the problems discussed by these rap artists.

The founding fathers of gangsta rap, such as Ice-T and the members of N.W.A., came from neighborhoods in Los Angeles plagued by violence associated with the drug trade. When asked about the violence in their lyrics, they typically argued that it was a direct reflection of violence that existed in reality. Ice-T, the father of gangsta rap and creator of the

Ice-T argues that his lyrics only reflect the realities of life in the ghetto.

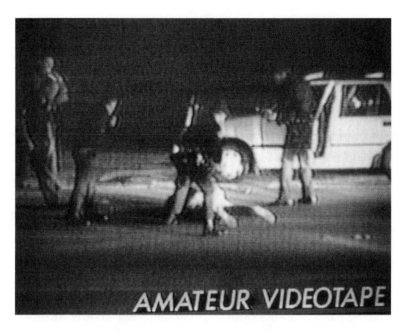

AMATEUR VIDEOTAPE

The Rodney King beating showed the American public that the violence depicted in rap music also existed in reality.

controversial speed metal song "Cop Killer," told reporters, "The way I rap, and what I rap about, is based in reality."[47] An executive for Time Warner, Owen Husney, agreed in a column he wrote for *Billboard* magazine in defense of the violent lyrics of his artists such as Ice-T. "Music is itself a reflection of the times," he wrote. "[Today] it's rap artists who reflect what's going on. It's groups like N.W.A., Ice Cube, and Ice-T who tell it like it is. You may not like everything they're saying because it's frighteningly real."[48]

In the late eighties and early nineties both Ice-T and N.W.A. made headlines for songs that were thought to encourage violence against police officers. When they tried to justify these songs or explain their anger toward the police, their arguments were dismissed by some, to whom they seemed unreasonable. These people did not believe that the police brutality described by N.W.A. and Ice-T actually existed and therefore did not understand the context of songs such as "Cop Killer" and "F___ Tha Police."

However, a few years later, videotapes surfaced that showed white Los Angeles police officers beating an African American man named Rodney King. Mainstream America now had visual evidence of the brutality that some African Americans had been facing at the hands of the police for years. "For nearly all black Angelenos, not to mention most inner-city residents, the videotaped beating of Rodney King was no surprise at all," wrote Robin D. G. Kelley in *The Nation*. "When L.A. rapper Ice Cube was asked about the King incident on MTV, he responded simply, 'It's been happening to us for years. It's just we didn't have a camcorder every time it happened.'"[49] Suddenly, gangsta rappers such as N.W.A. and Ice-T looked like prophets. "N.W.A. spoke of police brutality long before the Rodney King incident, but is anybody listening?"[50] wrote Owen Husney. Some people now realized that the violence depicted in some rap songs also existed in reality.

Telling it like it is or like it isn't?

Understanding that some lyrical violence was rooted in reality for some gangsta rap artists did not end criticism of these lyrics. While some critics conceded that a few original gangsta rap artists came from the streets and documented the experience of living in some of the poorest, most violent neighborhoods, they charged that now there were also impostors who were just in it for the money. "These lyrics depict ice-cold killers with gold chains swaggering in a desolate wasteland. This, [gangsta artists] argue, is the reality of their ghetto existence," *The Economist* magazine charged. "But their love affair with weapons, and the middle-class rappers who pretend to be gangsters, suggest that they are depicting violence for the sake of it."[51]

Original gangsta artists made music to express themselves and not necessarily for commercial gain, but after their success, other artists and executives knew that violent lyrics sold. Some people believed that savvy businesspeople had figured out a new way to sell records. Ian Steaman charged that "the horrific sells and that cloaking it under the guise of street reality legitimizes it."[52] In other words, Steaman believed some rap artists were not creating violent lyrics to express or document the grim reality of life, but instead were writing the most grotesquely violent lyrics they could think of just to sell records.

Nikki Giovanni, a poet and activist, defended violent lyrics and praised their authors for bringing attention to the violence that was an everyday fact of life for too many Americans. She stated that "rap is expressing the violence that's there, and we weren't even looking at that until rap came up and talked about it."[53] Others simply asserted that attacking the work of gangsta rappers was the wrong way to

Poet Nikki Giovanni praised rap artists for showing people that violence is a fact of life for many Americans.

go about solving the problem. "Given the theme of violence in the lyrics of some rap songs, there is concern that these songs rally America's youth to violent acts," critic Steve S. Salem wrote, but then added that "this is a case of attempting to treat the symptoms, not the cause. The argument is backward. By dealing with the actual violence on America's streets, artistic echoes of violence will diminish."[54]

Finally, some people saw the political attacks on violent lyrics as a way of distracting citizens from the actual problems in the United States. Tricia Rose states:

> Rap music has become a lightning rod for those politicians and law and order officials who are hell-bent on scapegoating it as a major source of violence instead of attending to the much more difficult and complicated work of transforming the brutally unjust institutions that shape the lives of poor people. Attacking rap during this so-called crisis of crime and violence is a . . . smokescreen that protects the real culprits and deludes the public into believing that public officials are taking a bite out of crime . . . [while] rappers are cast as the perpetrators.[55]

The violent deaths of gangsta rappers

While critics argued about the violent lyrics of gangsta rap, the real violence that plagued the lives of some gangsta rappers caught up with them. The lives of two very talented, young, influential gangsta rappers—Biggie Smalls (Notorious B.I.G.) and Tupac Shakur—ended far too soon. Both Smalls and Shakur were murdered in seemingly gang-related incidents similar to those they wrote about in their songs.

The death of these two rising stars of rap shook the industry to its core. While no one had anticipated such a violent end for these popular young men, some critics had warned that the "credentials" a rapper had to have to be considered "real" or "authentic" could lead to real trouble. Following the death of Eazy-E from AIDS, Michael Marriott pointed out that "Eazy-E was the first major rap star to die of AIDS, but not the first hard-core rapper to live out his own reckless lyrics celebrating the gangster lifestyle. Grammy Award–winning producer-rapper Dr. Dre is in a halfway house and rapper-actor Tupac Shakur is in jail, while reigning superstar Snoop Doggy Dogg

faces life in prison on conspiracy-murder charges, to which he pleaded not guilty.[56]

"In some twisted way criminal records have become the rap industry's requisite credentials of authenticity,"[57] Johnnie L. Roberts wrote in *Newsweek*. He was not the only one who noticed this trend. Even record executives such as Barry Weiss, senior vice president/general manager of Jive Records, had to admit that crime, jail time, and violent behavior were becoming prerequisites for gangsta rappers because "it [lent] added street credibility in a funny sort of way, which is bad."[58]

Critics, artists, and record executives worried about the violent lives of some gangsta rap stars in the years preceding the deaths of Biggie Smalls and Tupac Shakur in 1996, but the brutal murders of these two effectively marked the end—at

Tupac Shakur was murdered in a gang-related incident in 1996.

After the murders of Tupac Shakur and Biggie Smalls, Dr. Dre (pictured) began to denounce the violence portrayed in his lyrics.

least for a while—of gangsta rap. Gangsta artists still released records, but even the "father" of gangsta rap, Dr. Dre, seemed reformed by the senseless loss of two such talented individuals. He went on to denounce the violence in which his music had once reveled. Releasing a song titled "Been There, Done That," he made statements to the press in which he said he was not proud of his earlier actions. "I'm on a different page now," he told *Newsweek*. "I've done some wild and crazy s—t, s—t I'm not proud of. But I've grown up a lot in the last five years."[59] Dre went on to pronounce what he saw as the end of gangsta rap: "[gangsta rap's] run its course. . . . You're not going to get the sales talking the same old s—t."[60] Gangsta rap lay dormant for a few years until the late 1990s, when Dr. Dre teamed up with Marshall Mathers (Eminem) and released *The Slim Shady LP* that ignited debates over violence in rap music again.

4

Sexism

SEXISM, OR DISCRIMINATION against women, is a term found in numerous articles, books, and other reports on rap music. Rap has a long history of lyrics that critics found to be sexist, and an equally long history of being taken to task for those lyrics. Rap music was not the first—or the last—form of music to be cited as exhibiting this particular type of prejudice. Indeed, most other forms of popular music have been criticized for sexist lyrics. However, since the days of its inception, rap music has received an unprecedented amount of media attention for lyrics that some found offensive to women.

All about attitude

In the chorus of Ice Cube's "Don't Trust 'Em," the rapper insists that "bitches" can't be trusted. Since the derogatory term seemed to imply all women, such lyrics caused a great deal of debate both inside and outside the rap music industry. The controversy was only furthered when the term "ho" (short for whore) was also liberally used to describe the women portrayed in rap songs. Some critics, such as the staff of the magazine *The Economist*, believe the liberal and indiscriminate use of such offensive terms reveals an inherent sexism in the music. Citing this pervasive attitude, *The Economist* concluded, "Much of rap is misogynist [hateful toward women]. Women are seen as objects of lust, and devious gold-diggers."[6]

Artists, however, were quick to deny that they were equating "bitches" with all women. "On the album, I'm talking about particular types of women that I've met in my life [when the word 'bitch' or 'ho' is used]," Tha Dogg Pound's Ricardo "Kurupt" Brown said in response to criticism about the use of derogatory terms. "I have a mother, [female] cousins, and a baby by the way, so it's stupid to say [Tha Dogg Pound uses] 'bitches' and 'hoes' to talk about all women."[62] Brown's response is fairly typical. Quite a few rappers respond to charges of sexism by saying that disreputable women do in fact exist.

However, it is not the choice of words that is the issue for some critics, they are more concerned with the influence that negative terms such as these—and especially the constant rep-

The lyrics of Ice Cube's "Don't Trust 'Em" are full of terms that some listeners consider derogatory toward women.

etition of them—have on impressionable young men and women. They fear what the constant use of these terms teaches youth about the value of women in contemporary society. Bob DeMoss, the activist who led the charge against the Florida rap group 2 Live Crew, told *People* "to refer to women as bitches and whores 163 times [on an album] would inculcate the notion that in fact is what women are."[63]

John Leo takes a similar stance on 2 Live Crew, arguing that they packaged "the degradation of women . . . and beamed it to kids as entertainment."[64] The concern of critics such as Leo is that hearing women consistently referred to in a negative manner teaches young people that it is all right to do so because women have little value.

Abhorred by what she saw as the influence of gangsta rap music on young people in society, activist C. Delores Tucker told *People* magazine, "Little boys are calling little girls 'whores' because that's what they hear [in rap songs]."[65] Even average citizens worried about the effects of lyrics that were derogatory to women. "It's sad to see a young Black male hanging on the corner . . . calling a woman a 'bitch' or a 'ho,'"[66] one college student lamented in an interview with the *Black Collegian* about the influence of gangsta rap.

Some critics worry that the world of rap has developed to a point where gangsta rappers must be sexist in order to gain respect for their work. In an extensive essay on women in rap, Murray Forman asserts that "activities which often either ignore women or objectify and exploit them were, and in many cases still are widely regarded as being fundamental to the persona of some rappers and to the authenticity of the music."[67] In other words, Murray believes that in order to be considered an authentic hardcore rapper, an artist must degrade women.

Violence against women

Negative portrayals of women, degrading language, and the idea that demeaning women is an important part of being an authentic rapper are all things that critics fear influence individuals' opinions of women. However, of greater concern to some are rap lyrics in which violence toward women is celebrated. The N.W.A. song "One Less Bitch" is a graphic example of the kind of lyrics that have concerned critics. In the song, Dr. Dre raps that he does not like the way in which a prostitute performs, so he kills her. The lyrics explain that he tied her down, let his friends rape her, and then shot her with a handgun.

Angry that the protagonists of rap songs such as "One Less Bitch" rape and brutalize women in order to get revenge, Cardiss Collins, a representative for the State of Illi-

nois, told *Billboard* magazine, "Black women throughout the country 'are infuriated by the demeaning lyrics of this [gangsta rap] music that glorifies sexual harassment, sexual abuse, rape and murder of women.'"[68] Critics such as Collins worry that these sorts of rap lyrics glorify violence against women and desensitize listeners to this kind of violence. Worse yet, some people reason, this sort of desensitization can lead to actual violent acts against women.

Concerned about the effect of rap music on attitudes about violence toward women, some social scientists studied the effects of exposure to both violent and nonviolent rap music on young people. In a 1995 study, J. Johnson, L.A. Jackson, and L. Gatto "found that exposure to violent rap music did, in fact, tend to lead to a higher degree

Critics claim that rap songs like N.W.A.'s "One Less Bitch" celebrate and glamorize violence toward women. (Pictured are two actors performing a scene from the play 20-52.)

of acceptance of the use of violence (including violence against women)."[69] However, a second study by James D. Johnson, Mike S. Adams, Leslie Ashburn, and William Reed found that rap music did not necessarily even have to be violent to convey the message that violence against women was acceptable. Their 1995 study found that "female subjects who were exposed to the [nonviolent rap] videos reported greater acceptance of teen dating violence than females who were not exposed to the videos."[70] In other words, negative images of women alone can affect young girls' attitudes about tolerating violence toward women.

Censoring sexism

"Why," asks John Leo, "should our daughters have to grow up in a culture in which musical advice on the domination and abuse of women is accepted as entertainment?"[71] Leo's question came as part of his essay in *U.S. News & World Report* arguing for an end to such sexist lyrics in rap music.

When people such as Leo started calling for the removal, or some sort of censorship, of sexist lyrics, others leapt to the defense of rap artists. These individuals believed that—purposefully or not—the extreme sexism in some songs only succeeded in making being a sexist look silly. Henry Louis Gates Jr. wrote "Luther Campbell's [of 2 Live Crew] outlandish display of black macho made sexism look silly and repellent, not attractive."[72]

Others asserted that rappers were being unfairly targeted. These defenders admitted the existence of sexist phrases in some rap music, and vehemently disagreed with these lyrics. However, they added that rap music was not alone in this arena and reminded people that popular music has a long history of sexism. "Some responses to sexism in rap music adopt a tone that suggests rappers have infected an otherwise sexism-free society," Tricia Rose wrote. "Rap's sexist lyrics are . . . part of a rampant and viciously normalized sexism that dominates the . . . music business."[73]

Women and the music industry

Some critics suggest that sexism in rap music has gone unchecked because very few women have been able to break into the world of rap music. Whether it's rock and roll, country, or hip hop, the music industry is dominated by men who do most of the signing of acts, recording, producing, marketing,

Defenders of sexist lyrics argue that the macho attitudes of Luther Campbell and other rappers make sexism look silly.

and owning. Rap is no exception. In the early days of rap, female acts were actually fairly common, but as rap became a big-money enterprise they slowly disappeared. Murray Forman explains what happened to these pioneering women: "Most failed to win major record deals and were subsequently reduced to the role of opening acts on live concert bills. Unable to sustain themselves on the meager income from live engagements . . . many promising female rappers faded from the scene."[74] By the early eighties there were very few successful female artists, and this, combined with the negative images of women in some songs, left critics questioning the rap music industry. Some suggested that more positive images of women would appear in lyrics if there were more female rappers, and they wondered precisely what was keeping women out of the rap scene.

The record label Jive's senior vice president and general manager Barry Weiss argued that rap's audience caused the absence of women. "In terms of who buys the records and dictates the tastes, rap is male-dominated," he told *Billboard*. "There's a place for female rappers, but for them to happen they've almost got to be twice as good as a male."[75] Female rappers did begin to reemerge in the mid-eighties, and the commercial success of some female artists made labels less wary of signing women. However, female rappers with recording contracts were still few and far between.

Weiss's line of thinking—that the rap audience only wants male rappers—is shared by many within the music industry, and some critics argue that it is actually this attitude—and not rap's audience—that has shut women out. "Since a macho image is a proven formula for success, rap producers were reluctant to sign female acts,"[76] wrote David Thigpen. Obviously, if women are not signed to contracts, they cannot sell records. Still, a recording contract is only the first step on the road to becoming a successful recording artist; Queen Latifah spoke about the ways in which being a woman made subsequent steps such as promotion and marketing more difficult as well. "People wonder why girls don't go platinum [sell over a million records], but a lot of the time we don't get the same money [that men do for marketing and promotion], and that's just a straight-up fact."[77]

Singer Lauryn Hill is one of many female artists who had trouble breaking into the music industry.

Women are not only underrepresented in the ranks of rap artists. Those who wish to work on the technical side and be DJs or producers also confront barriers solely because they are women. Some of this is the result of prevailing attitudes within the industry. Recently, hip hop's Lauryn Hill spoke about the difficulties she had confronting these attitudes when she wanted to produce:

> When [they saw a] woman step into the studio . . . I think they sort of looked at me kind of funny . . . and it took for me to play some of the music I'd already done for them to warm up to me giving them direction. You know it's not an easy thing for . . . a woman to be in charge [as a producer] because I think there's not an initial, immediate respect that's given. There's automatically . . . a sort of question.[78]

The scarcity of women rappers, producers, and even record executives has made it difficult for women to counteract the preponderance of negative images of females in rap lyrics with positive ones, critics charge. However, some of the female rappers who have broken through were able to do just that.

Women take the mike

Despite the obstacles they faced from sexism within the music industry, by the mid-eighties some female rap acts began to achieve success through sheer determination. The first female rappers to really make it big were Cheryl James (Salt) and Sandy Denton (Pepa) of Salt 'N' Pepa. Tricia Rose explains the key role these two women played in rap music:

> It is difficult to ignore the massive increase in record deals for women rappers following Salt 'N' Pepa's double platinum (2 million) 1986 debut album *Hot, Cool and Vicious*. Such volume sales, even for a rap album by a male artist, were virtually [unheard of] in 1986. Since then, several female rappers . . . have finally been recorded and promoted.[79]

This dynamic duo was followed by women such as Queen Latifah, MC Lyte, Missy "Misdemeanor" Elliot, Li'l Kim, and Lauryn Hill, who have also sold a great many albums.

Some of these successful women did directly challenge the sexist lyrics of their male counterparts. For instance, while Pepa refused to criticize male rappers for lyrics that portrayed women as "whores" and "gold diggers," she also pointed out that Salt 'N' Pepa's "job" was to counteract these negative images of women. "What we're doing is sharing the things we've witnessed regarding some men's treatment of women, trying to set an example of independence, and let women know they shouldn't be giving those guys so much to talk about,"[80] she told *Billboard* magazine.

In her lyrics for her song "U.N.I.T.Y." Queen Latifah spoke out against the negative images of women and demanded respect. CeCe McGhee of WUSL radio in Philadelphia told *Billboard* about the effect the single had on the local rap scene. "Since 'U.N.I.T.Y.' has come out, I've seen a lot of women out there who used to be ho-hum about derogatory la-

bels of women now vocalizing their dislike of the references.
. . Where it was once easy for local rappers to put in words
like 'ho' and 'bitch' into their lyrics, now they're paying closer
attention."[1]

Some critics have even suggested that the rap music industry is unique and allows female rappers to deal with sexism more effectively than women can in any other genre.
"To some extent women deal with sexism much more directly in rap than in other musical genres," Lucy O'Brien
wrote in her book *She-Bop*. "The posturing male attitudes
they face are so upfront and overt that arguably this allows
them to be serious about their music and how they present
themselves. In an area like street rap they cannot afford to
be covert, and the sexuality they project is not coy and dis-
creet."[8] However, just because a rapper is female does not
necessarily mean that she is against sexism in rap music,

Despite the industry's history of being male-dominated, many female rap acts such as Salt 'N' Pepa have been able to achieve success.

and sometimes she may even be sexist herself. Tricia Rose reminds her readers that just as there are male rappers whose lyrics are antisexist, so too are there female rappers whose lyrics reinforce sexist notions. She points out that "their lyrics sometimes affirm patriarchal notions about family life and the traditional roles of husbands, fathers, and lovers."[83]

Female rappers who attacked sexism did so not only in their lyrics. Some were also living, breathing, positive images of womanhood for their fans. Murray Forman noted this, stating, "Through their public presence and articulation, [female rappers] have provided influential role models for an entire generation of female fans."[84] Some women, most notably Queen Latifah, even worked to get more women into

Queen Latifah's attempts to help female rap artists succeed is just one way that women have countered rap's sexist attitudes.

the business. *Billboard* magazine's Havelock Nelson reported on this phenomenon. "With her own label and management firm, Latifah has become one of few women icons in the rap world," he wrote. "But she isn't the only artist spearheading the careers of others. In fact, many of the new female MCs have gotten a leg up from established [female] acts."[85] This sort of sponsorship is just one of the ways that women have fought against sexism in the rap music industry as well as in rap lyrics. However, even though there are more females in the business, and more positive images of women have been recorded, their fight is ongoing.

5

Prejudice

BECAUSE RAP LYRICS tend to have more words than an average pop song, artists have a venue to tell complex stories and send complete messages. While the messages of many songs are positive, artists have been criticized for presenting messages that some people believed were negative and even dangerous.

Sexism was one such prejudicial message that concerned some, but it was by no means the only one. Throughout rap's history, specific artists have been charged with endorsing anti-Semitism, homophobia, racism, or antiwhite sentiments in their lyrics. As rap's popularity grew by leaps and bounds from the late eighties to the present, some songs had lyrics that were thought to encourage prejudice, which was especially troublesome given rap's ever-expanding audience. As a result, critics challenged their lyrics. Criticisms, which were typically presented in the press, at times put pressure on artists forcing them to change their ways. But usually, they did very little to alter an artist's behavior or a record label's willingness to sell objectionable records.

The Public Enemy showdown over anti-Semitism

Public Enemy was one of the first rap groups to be taken to task for lyrics perceived of as prejudiced. The group was composed of rappers Carlton Ridenhour (Chuck D) and William Drayton (Flavor Flav), DJ Norman Rogers (DJ Terminator X), and Robert Griffen (Professor Griff), who was the group's "minister of information" and headed up the Security of the First World Dancers, Public Enemy's backup dancers who wore paramilitary garb. They worked with their production team called the Bomb Squad (Hank Shocklee, Keith Shocklee, Bill Stepheny, and Eric Sadler) to become one of the pioneering rap groups—both sonically and politically. Public Enemy put their pro–black nationalist ideology into their music and in so doing, became one of the first rap groups to achieve widespread popularity while being overtly political. Public Enemy songs such as "Bring the Noise," "Don't Believe the Hype," and "Fight the Power" made them a favorite with young people from all walks of life even though they showcased a pro-black sentiment.

Public Enemy was one of the first rap groups accused of promoting racial prejudice.

However, as this revolutionary group approached the peak of its success, they hit a roadblock. Professor Griff, who did not perform musically in Public Enemy, made comments to the *Washington Times* that set off a public relations nightmare for the group. A columnist for *The Nation*, Gene Santoro, described the incident: "Professor Griff parroted a Louis Farrakhan [leader of the Nation of Islam, a black nationalist organization] line of anti-Semitism during an interview . . . on May 22, 1989, saying, 'Jews are wicked . . . [and responsible for] the majority of wickedness that goes on across the globe.'"[86] Griff went on to make further derogatory comments about Jewish people, and when the article appeared, a good number of people were upset by his comments. They also worried about the influence such comments might have on the beliefs of Public Enemy's listeners.

Jewish organizations sent letters of protest to Public Enemy's record label. People passed out flyers with Griff's comments written on them in hopes that it would discourage people from purchasing the group's albums as well as retailers from carrying them. Columnists, critics, and pundits began calling for the removal of Professor Griff from the group, and Rabbi Abraham Cooper, a Jewish rights activist, launched a nationwide advertising campaign to bring attention to Griff's bigotry. The ad appeared in newspapers across the country, including the *New York Times*, and denounced Public Enemy for its bigotry. On the other hand were critics who came to Public Enemy's defense. They saw Griff's remarks as part and parcel of his Farrakhan-inspired ideology and argued that this very same ideology had also been an extremely positive, empowering force in Public Enemy's music.

Public pressure

As the media pressure mounted and cries for Griff's removal became louder, "It got to the point where people did not want to take pictures, or be associated with the group Public Enemy,"[87] recalled Hank Shocklee. Chuck D was urged by an angry public to take action. He called a press conference and told reporters:

Rabbi Abraham Cooper's nationwide campaign against Public Enemy was a response to Professor Griff's anti-Semitic comments.

The black community is in crisis. Our mission as musicians is to address these problems. Offensive remarks by Professor Griff are not in line with Public Enemy's program. We are not anti-Jewish. We are pro-black, pro–black culture, and pro–human race. Griff was to transmit these values. He sabotaged this.[88]

Chuck D went on to say that Griff was suspended from the group. Shortly thereafter, Chuck D reinstated Griff and disbanded Public Enemy. According to Chuck D, this was his way of boycotting the music industry that he felt had pressured him into firing Griff. However, when Griff then made disparaging comments about other members of Public

Written by Chuck D (left), Public Enemy's song "Welcome to the Terrordome" contains phrases that have been called anti-Semitic.

Enemy in subsequent interviews, he was thrown out of the group for good and Public Enemy began to work again.

Griff's final removal from the group satisfied critics, who believed it was a sign that Public Enemy had taken an aggressive stance against anti-Semitism within their own ranks. These same critics were sorely disappointed when the group's first post-Griff song appeared in 1989. The song, "Welcome to the Terrordome," was penned by Chuck D and seemed to some to be a defense of Griff's statements. The song also contained phrases such as "crucifixion ain't no fiction," "they got me like Jesus," and "told a Rab get off the rag"[89] that were interpreted by some critics as anti-Semitic. Now, Chuck D was being accused of anti-Semitism. He responded to these accusations, but as Alan Light recalls in *The Vibe History of Hip Hop,* "His explanations were just barely acceptable. Even if his intentions weren't malicious, he had to know the effect these words would have with the spotlight so squarely on his next move post-Griff."[90]

Slowly but surely the media frenzy surrounding the lyrics of "Welcome to the Terrordome" calmed down, thanks in part to the fact that no more anti-Semitic comments were made by group members. With this behind them, Public Enemy moved forward. Although the criticism of Griff's anti-Semitic remarks had led to his removal from the group, Public Enemy's post-Griff songs still managed to climb into the top ten and the group enjoyed a fair amount of success in his absence. However, the story of Griff's anti-Semitic comments, how they affected the group, and Chuck D's "Welcome to the Terrordome" lyrics live on as some of the most infamous examples of prejudice in the world of rap music.

Antiwhite sentiment

Public Enemy's anti-Semitism offended the Jewish community and its supporters. Other people have also been offended by rap music on the basis of race. Some music industry insiders attest to the fact that antiwhite sentiment is fairly commonplace in rap lyrics and the rap music industry. Nelson George testified to this in *Hip Hop America* when he wrote, "Antiwhite rhetoric flows through hip hop." However, while everyday anger at white society or even antiwhite sentiments may be common in rap, there have also been times when rap artists have been accused of crossing the line and being too antiwhite. In such cases, their lyrics or public statements were, in the minds of some critics, antiwhite to such a degree that they stirred debate in the media as well as the rap music industry.

In the early days of rap there was a small group of rappers whose political beliefs resulted in lyrics that were antiwhite. They were members of a political and religious group called Five Percenters, an offshoot of the Nation of Islam, and had lyrics that stated that white people were devils. Five Percent rappers such as Rakim, Lakim Shabazz, and the Poor Righteous Teachers never gained widespread popularity, but George points out that they left behind a legacy. "In much of hip hop, the Five Percenter belief that white men are devils . . . and that black men are Gods here on earth echoes as loudly as a drum sample,"[1] he writes.

Other, rappers have also been taken to task for their antiwhite lyrics or comments that caused a great deal more controversy. Sister Souljah was one such rapper, but the

Sister Souljah's celebrity rose briefly when Bill Clinton interpreted her comments as being antiwhite.

extent of the controversy had more to do with who criticized her than her comments themselves. In the wake of the 1992 Los Angeles riots, she told the *Washington Post,* "I mean, if black people kill black people every day, why not have a week and kill white people?"[92] Sister Souljah's comments were interpreted by Bill Clinton, then a presidential candidate, to be antiwhite. When he said as much to the press, Sister Souljah became an instant household name. However, Martin Johnson points out that this did very little for Sister Souljah's recording career. "Although the . . . controversy landed Souljah on the cover of *Newsweek,* her debut album, *360 Degrees of Power,* was released that summer and tanked."[93] Thus, the controversy amounted to her brief moment of fame.

More established, mainstream, popular rap artists have also faced a torrent of media criticism for voicing antiwhite sentiments. In 1997, Grammy Award in hand for her work with the Fugees, Lauryn Hill made comments to the press that were construed by some to be antiwhite. She told reporters that she hoped only African Americans would purchase Fugee albums. Biographer Marc Shapiro explained the subsequent fallout:

> Word spread like wildfire about Lauryn's "racist" remarks. Pras and Wyclef [the two other members of the Fugees] . . . did their best to mollify [calm down] the growing backlash against the group. . . . Lauryn would backtrack in subsequent interviews, stating that what she had said was misinterpreted.[94]

Hill also told reporters that she did not have hate for anybody. Whether or not a person believes Hill's statement was antiwhite, one thing is for certain—it did not hurt record sales. The Fugees second album, *The Score,* was out at the time and continued to sell at a record pace.

Minority bashing

When African American rappers make antiwhite statements, a minority group is attacking the majority. But there are also instances where African American rap artists have made prejudiced statements about other racial minorities. Ice Cube (O'Shea Jackson) began his career with the Los

Critics claimed that the lyrics in Ice Cube's song "Black Korea" promoted violence against Koreans.

Angeles gangsta rap group N.W.A., but it was as a solo artist that he released the controversial song "Black Korea." The song was released roughly eight months after a Los Angeles Korean grocer, Soon Ja Du, shot and killed a teenage African American girl in a dispute over a bottle of juice. In November 1991, Du received a suspended sentence for his actions and many people were outraged.

In Ice Cube's song, the protagonist threatens Korean merchants that if they do not respect African Americans, their stores will be burned down. The staff of *Billboard* magazine thought that Ice Cube had crossed the line here on *Death Certificate*. "It seems to us that Ice Cube's lyrics express the rankest sort of racism and hatemongering," their November 23, 1991, editorial read. "His unabashed espousal of violence against Koreans . . . crosses the line that divides art from advocacy of crime."[95] When the L.A. riots broke out and more than two thousand Korean businesses were destroyed, the song seemed all the more prejudiced and dangerous. Critic Mortimer B. Zuckerman cited it as evidence of "a growing racism in black communities towards Asians and other minorities."[96]

Homophobia

One group of people that, until recently, rap artists have gotten relatively little flak for preaching prejudice against is gays and lesbians. Quite a few critics note that homophobia is a staple of many rap songs. "Homophobia . . . [is] often inextricable from 'authentic' hip-hop,"[97] writes Stephen Rodrick in *The New Republic*. However, as Eric Dyson points out, these are typically comments made in passing, and even the most vocal critics of rap rarely speak out about its homophobia. During a time when politicians were documenting the evils of gangsta rap, Dyson wrote:

> I am wholly sympathetic, for instance, to sharp criticism of gangsta rap's ruinous sexism and homophobia, though neither [Senator Bob] Dole, [William] Bennett nor [activist C. Delores] Tucker has made much of the latter plague. Perhaps that's because there's an implicit agreement between gangsta rappers and political elites that gays, lesbians and bisexuals basically deserve what they get.[98]

However, some rap artists have changed their tune as a result of either information or pressure from the gay community. For instance, Ice-T eliminated antigay messages from his work. "I used to make fun of gay people, call them fags," he told *Time* magazine. "But my homeys weren't down with that, so now I lay off."[99] But Ice-T is the exception instead of the rule. In fact, there is a long history in rap music of artists who have sold and continue to sell millions of records despite—or because of—their homophobic lyrics.

Recently, rapper Eminem (Marshall Mathers) met with a great deal of criticism for some lyrics on his album *The Marshall Mathers LP*. The Gay Lesbian Alliance Against Defamation (GLAAD) objected to lyrics that used violent images to emphasize his dislike for gays and lesbians. They issued a press release, an alert, in regard to the album. "Eminem's lyrics are soaked with violence and full of negative comments about many groups, including lesbians and gay men," the GLAAD alert reads. "While Eminem certainly has the freedom of speech to rap whatever he wants, it is irresponsible for UNI/Interscope Records as a company to produce and promote such defamatory material that encourages violence and hatred. This is especially negligent when considering the market for this music has been shown to be adolescent males, the very group that statistically commits the most hate crimes."[100]

In conjunction with the alert, GLAAD staged a protest of Eminem's onstage appearance at the MTV music video awards. As a result, they got MTV to capitulate to running a public service message after Eminem's performance that discouraged the hatred of gay, lesbian, and bisexual men and women. For his part, Eminem has responded to numerous reporters about the homophobia of his lyrics. "Let me ask you this: Has anybody went out yet and bashed a gay person when they listened to my record?" he asked Anthony DeCurtis who interviewed him for *Rolling Stone*. "Has there been a case? So what's the point? The term 'f----t' doesn't necessarily mean a gay person. To me, it don't. Everybody uses that f----g word. It's just that I'm selling millions of records, so people are coming down on me."[101]

The interesting thing about the debates regarding prejudiced lyrics is that neither side argues that the prejudice does not exist. The majority of critics agree that these sorts of lyrics or offensive statements by performers are bad news for rap music and its listeners. Some try to excuse the lyrics, others dismiss them, still others argue that they should not be allowed to be recorded, marketed, or sold because of the influence they have on young people. "Whether we like it or not musicians, rock stars, and all the rest, they're icons to young people. They always have been and they always will be," Rabbi Cooper stated when asked why he began a campaign against Professor Griff's anti-Semitic remarks. "[That's why]

Eminem's songs have been accused of containing lyrics that are homophobic.

in a sense, it's more troubling to hear [bigotry] come out of the mouth of a young musician."[102] This, then, is where the discussion of prejudice in rap music lyrics ends and the censorship debate begins, because while some people believe that artists should be stopped from preaching prejudice, others believe that taking action against them amounts to censorship.

6

Rap and Censorship

SOME CRITICS CALL rap music sexist, others contend it glorifies or causes violence, and the lyrics of some songs are seen as anti-Semitic, racist, homophobic, or otherwise prejudiced. Believing that many of these songs send harmful messages, some critics call for record companies, musicians, or the government to place restrictions on what artists can say in their lyrics. Others contend that such controls amount to censorship.

The first amendment and censorship

Unfortunately, censorship is very difficult to understand because people have very different ideas about what it is and what it is not. In the United States, the definition of censorship typically hinges upon the interpretation of the First Amendment to the Constitution. Among other things, the First Amendment states that "Congress shall make no law . . . abridging the freedom of speech." Some people believe this should mean that citizens can say whatever they want, wherever they want to do so. However, others firmly believe the First Amendment was written to protect *most* types of speech, and that there should be limits on certain types of speech that may have no political or artistic value—such as hate speech or pornography.

Parents' Music Resource Center

In 1985 Tipper Gore, wife of then-senator Al Gore, became outraged by the music her children were listening to. Using her political influence, Gore teamed up with Susan

Baker, wife of then-treasury secretary James A. Baker III, and together they founded the Parents' Music Resource Center (PMRC). The PMRC wanted some authority—either the record companies themselves or Congress—to put some controls or limitations on the lyrics of music that children could purchase. They brought public and political attention to the lyrics of songs they found to be objectionable, gained supporters, and began to pressure Congress to enact legislation to restrict the sale of songs with objectionable lyrics to minors [people under the age of eighteen]. Responding to pressure from the PMRC in combination with the National Parent Teacher Association, the Senate held an "information only" hearing about pop song lyrics that the PMRC deemed vile and profane.

Since these hearings were "information only," no laws were passed to force record companies to take any protective measures. However, the hearings created a great deal of public and political pressure that compelled the Recording Industry Association of America (RIAA) to "voluntarily" do so. Some music industry insiders—represented by the RIAA— believed it was inevitable that legislation would eventually be passed if they did not take action. In the end, the RIAA reached an agreement with the National Parent Teacher Association to place "parental advisory" stickers on music with explicit or violent lyrics.

Almost immediately following the creation of the advisory sticker, some of the nation's largest retailers such as K-Mart and Wal-Mart, as well as many smaller businesses, refused to carry any albums that were labeled. Record companies responded by producing "clean" versions of albums on which objectionable lyrics are bleeped out. Consumers then had a choice of which version of the album they wished to purchase.

However, there are critics who believe that the parental advisory label represents an attempt to limit speech, and thereby infringes upon freedom of speech. Some argue that the PMRC's labeling system is a form of censorship because it makes it impossible to obtain the original "unclean" version of albums in parts of the country where retailers refuse to carry them. They assert that in cases such as these, people are denied access to "information," and that amounts to censorship.

Other critics come at the free speech issue from a different angle. They maintain that since the industry knows objectionable music will be labeled and perhaps not sold by major retailers, artists and record companies often censor music before it is released so that it will be available for sale everywhere. This is precisely the charge that Howie Klein, president of Reprise Records, recently leveled against the parental advisory sticker when he told the *LA Times* that "it affects what artists record and who the record companies sign."[103]

As Nasty as They Wanna Be

Public outrage over the profanity found on 2 Live Crew's album As Nasty as They Wanna Be *led to its removal from record stores in Florida.*

Some rap musicians and songs were involved in the "information only" hearings before the Senate. However, the hearings predominantly focused on rock and roll and heavy metal. It was not until the late eighties and early nineties that rap began to feel the effects of the PMRC and the politics surrounding objectionable lyrics as many hardcore rappers' lyrics drew their ire.

At the forefront of the censorship debate was a then-unknown rap group called 2 Live Crew. Their 1990 album, *As Nasty as They Wanna Be*, sparked a heated debate that went beyond the mere labeling of objectionable material. When 2 Live Crew released the album, some people were outraged by its lyrics, which contained a lot of profanity, and wanted to halt the sale of the album. Organizations began to circulate transcripts of the lyrics of *As Nasty as They Wanna Be,* and in Florida a lawyer named Jack Thompson sent the lyrics to the governor and all the Florida sheriffs. Broward County sheriff Nick Navarro got a judge to rule that the lyrics of *As Nasty as They Wanna Be* were "probably obscene." He then dispatched his forces to warn shop owners that if they did not remove it from their shelves, they would be arrested. The band sued, and Florida governor Bob Martinez pushed for an investigation.

In March 1990 *Time* magazine told its readers what was going on in Florida and even offered an explanation as to why Governor Martinez was involved:

> Hurt by the collapse of an attempt to increase restrictions on abortions and an image of indecisiveness, Florida's Republican Governor Bob Martinez will have trouble winning a second term. He is trying to boost his chances by leaping on an unlikely issue. He has asked the state prosecutor to bring obscenity . . . charges against a popular rap-music band, the 2 Live Crew, for recording an album whose title, *As Nasty As They Wanna Be*, aptly describes its contents.[104]

Eventually, U.S. District Court judge Jose Gonzalez Jr. declared the record obscene. This was the first time in the history of popular music in the United States that a sound recording received legal censure. This ruling led to the arrest of a record shop owner named Charles Freeman for selling the album as well as half of the members of 2 Live Crew, who were arrested for performing songs from the album at an adults-only show.

Debates erupted in the press. Some critics charged that 2 Live Crew was being made an example of because they were an easy target—a small rap group with no major label support. Others maintained that the events in Florida were a freedom of speech issue with a racial twist. They argued that there were equally offensive recordings by white performers that were not declared obscene or even under attack. Dave Marsh, editor of the newsletter *Rock & Roll Confidential,* told *People* that

"what [this] is about is who has the right to speak in America
. . . and whether or not people who have non-Euro-American
values and nonfundamentalist Christian values have the right
to speak in language that like-minded individuals will understand. It's about the First Amendment."[105]

However, those who did not want 2 Live Crew's lyrics to
be available for sale believed its defenders were misinformed.
"Liberals discuss 2 Live Crew as if it posed only a First
Amendment problem," read an editorial in the *National Review*. "Liberals may want to pretend it's somehow art for art's
sake. It's more nearly crime for crime's sake."[106]

Ironically, Martinez's bid to stop the sale of *As Nasty as
They Wanna Be* accomplished just the opposite. The press focused on the controversy in Florida and as a result 2 Live
Crew achieved national recognition. Album sales skyrock-
eted, and the group enjoyed its first multi-platinum album.
Producers and rap artists took notice because controversy
generated sales. Eventually, the obscenity ruling was reversed
in a higher court and the charges against 2 Live Crew and

Freeman were dropped. However, while *As Nasty as They Wanna Be* was no longer legally considered obscene, this was not the last time that rap music and its censorship would be used by politicians to attract voters.

"Cop Killer"

Even though Bob Martinez's stance against the lyrics of 2 Live Crew failed to win him the 1990 Florida gubernatorial election, rap lyrics remained a political battleground. The artist or song at the center of the debate continued to change, but politicians running for office on either the state or the federal level began to let their views on rap be known. Nowhere was this more evident than in the 1992 campaign for the presidency between George Bush, Bill Clinton, and Ross Perot, in which each of the candidates spoke out about the lyrics of at least one rap song.

The artist originally at the center of the debate was Ice-T. In the late eighties, Ice-T put gangster rap on the map with his

In 1992 Ice-T became the center of controversy after releasing the song "Cop Killer."

debut album, *Rhyme Pays*. While this album drew a great deal of criticism for profanity, glorifications of crime, violence, sexism, and homophobia, it was the release of the album *Body Count* with Ice-T's speed metal band of the same name that ignited a political maelstrom.

The album was released at a time when tensions were already high between the police and African Americans. In the spring of 1992 the verdict was handed down in the trial of three white police officers who had been videotaped beating a black suspect by the name of Rodney King. The officers were found not guilty, and many people believed this was a miscarriage of justice. Subsequently riots erupted in Los Angeles, where the beating had taken place.

Rodney King speaks at a press conference following the acquittal of the LAPD officers accused of beating him.

In this charged atmosphere, Ice-T released the song "Cop Killer" on the album *Body Count*. According to Ice-T, the song was written from the perspective of a black man who becomes so enraged at his mistreatment by the police that he goes out with a gun to kill cops. Some law enforcement officials worried that "Cop Killer" would lead some of its listeners to try to unleash their own rage and shoot real police officers.

The song is not a rap song, but those who opposed it referred frequently to "Cop Killer" as a rap song in the press. Perhaps this was because rapper Ice-T recorded it and people had difficulty defining rap, but Ice-T suggests that referring to "Cop Killer" as a rap song was a calculated political move on the part of those who opposed it. "Politically, they know by saying the word *rap* they can get a lot of people who think, 'Rap-black-rap-black-ghetto,' and don't like it."[107] Whatever the reason, the American public came to associate "Cop Killer" with rap music, and as the debate over the song heated up, rap music lyrics became an issue in the 1992 presidential campaign.

Presidents, presidential hopefuls, and gangstas

The Combined Law Enforcement Associations of Texas called a press conference to call for a boycott of Time Warner, the parent company of Ice-T's record label, Sire, that produced *Body Count*. "You mix this with the summer, the violence and a little drugs," Doug Elder, president of the Houston Police Officers' Association offered as a reason for the boycott, "and they [Ice-T, Sire, and Time Warner] are going to unleash a reign of terror on communities all across the country."[108]

Joined by the PMRC and numerous other organizations, the boycott of all Time Warner products proceeded. Boycotters urged retailers not to sell the album and hoped to force Time Warner to halt the sale of *Body Count* until "Cop Killer" was removed from the album. *Billboard* magazine contended that boycotters were essentially using the police to force Time Warner to censor their artist. "The threat of a Time Warner boycott led by law enforcement authorities constitutes intimidation, if not outright censorship," they editorialized.

After much pressure from the public and President Bush, Ice-T announced the removal of the controversial song "Cop Killer" from his album Body Count.

However, this was not anything particularly new. After all, N.W.A.'s antipolice song, "F___ Tha Police" had caused a similar controversy in1989. But the "Cop Killer" controversy took the lyrics and censorship debate to a whole new political level when President George Bush told reporters that Ice-T was "sick" and Time Warner was "wrong" to release the album. Vice President Dan Quayle and other conservatives joined Bush in condemning "Cop Killer," those who created it, and those who released it.

Billboard magazine suggested that this was a savvy political move. "The debate over *Body Count*'s output is a convenient campaign detour," read the July 18 editorial. "Incumbent conservatives are stoking the controversy in hopes that a hypnotized public will forget such pressing issues as massive unemployment, homelessness, environmental pollution, and government corruption."[109] In the end, Ice-T bowed to political pressure and pulled "Cop Killer" from his album, telling reporters, "It's my fight, not a Warner Bros. fight."[110] Still, Bush's stance on "Cop Killer" made it—and rap music in general—an issue in the campaign for the presidency. Soon other candidates also took a stance, and as the debate spread to other politicians, it spread to other rap musicians, and this time real rap songs.

Political targets

Presidential hopeful Ross Perot went on record in agreement with Bush about "Cop Killer," while Quayle moved on to criticize Tupac (2Pac) Shakur. Shakur's album, *2Pacalypse Now*, contained songs such as "I Don't Give a F___," in which the narrator was critical of police brutality and took violent action against law enforcement officials. The album itself was named in a lawsuit brought by the family of a Texas state trooper who was shot by a young man listening to the album. "There is absolutely no reason for a record like this to be published by a responsible corporation," Quayle said, taking aim at Time Warner, which released *2Pacalypse Now*. "I am suggesting that [the record label] withdraw this record. It has no place in our society."[111]

Congress jumps on board

With presidential candidates successfully taking stands against rap songs on a national level, state and local politicians began to do so as well. Sixty members of Congress wrote letters and petitioned Time Warner to remove "Cop Killer" from *Body Count*. However, in 1994, Congress became far more involved in dealing with the lyrics of rap music at the urging of C. Delores Tucker, chairwoman of the National Political Congress of Black Women, and William Bennett of Empower America.

The alliance of these two individuals was political in and of itself. Tucker was a liberal activist who had been part of the civil rights movement, and Bennett was a very conservative Republican. However, on the issue of gangsta rap they agreed—it had to be cleaned up. Together they worked to get a hearing with the Committee on Energy and Commerce's Subcommittee on Commerce, Competitiveness, and Consumer Protection. The purpose of these hearings was to investigate "production, sale, and distribution . . . of music that is alleged to contain lyrics that are violent, misogynistic, and homophobic."[112] These hearings gave members of Congress an opportunity to speak their minds about rap music. No official sanctions or laws came out of these hearings, but they showed just how political the control/censorship of rap lyrics had become.

The political furor over lyrics and their censorship died down when rap artists moved away from gangsta rap in the late nineties following the deaths of Biggie Smalls and Tupac Shakur. It laid dormant for a few years, only to be brought back to life and placed on the political docket once again. The

C. Delores Tucker, a liberal, civil rights activist, discusses the negative effects of gangsta rap's violent lyrics.

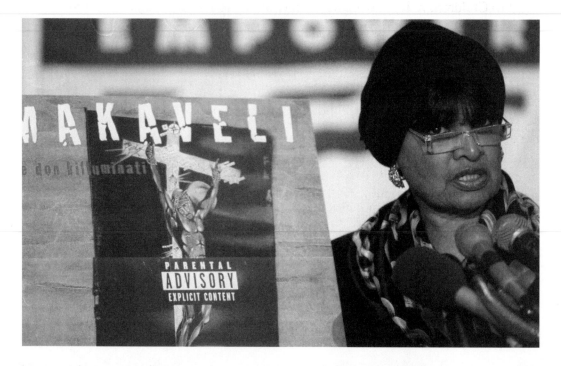

effects of violent lyrics on children were discussed following the April 19, 1999, events at Columbine High School in Colorado. On this day, two of the school's students went on a shooting spree, killing thirteen people and wounding more than twenty before taking their own lives. In an effort to find answers, President Bill Clinton asked the Federal Trade Commission (FTC) to investigate the marketing of violent entertainment to children.

In September 2000 the FTC released its report and made a prepared statement before the Senate Committee on Commerce, Science, and Transportation titled "Marketing Violent Entertainment to Children: A Review of Self-Regulation and Industry Practices in the Motion Picture, Music Recording, and Electronic Game Industries." The report concluded that violent entertainment—including violent music lyrics—was indeed being marketed to children and suggested that the entertainment industry impose sanctions on companies that engage in such practices. The FTC report represents a shift in focus in the censorship debate. Lawmakers and activists seem to have moved away from attempting to stop the distribution and sale of music with questionable lyrics and instead are focusing on record companies' marketing of these lyrics to young people. Whether this new focus will quell the debate or fan the flames further remains to be seen.

After the 1999 shootings at Columbine High School, President Clinton ordered an investigation into the marketing of violent entertainment to children.

Notes

Introduction

1. Quoted in David Gates with Peter Katel, "The Importance of Being Nasty," *Newsweek*, July 2, 1990, p. 52.

2. Quoted in Gates, "The Importance of Being Nasty," p. 52.

3. Christopher Hitchens, "Minority Report," *The Nation*, July 30–August 6, 1990, p. 120.

4. Hitchens, "Minority Report," p. 120.

5. Tricia Rose, *Black Noise: Rap Music and Black Culture in Contemporary America*. Hanover, NH: Wesleyan University Press, 1994, p. 2.

Chapter 1: The Originality of Reconstructed Music

6. Rose, *Black Noise*, p. 2.

7. Nelson George, *Buppies, B-Boys, Baps, & Bohos: Notes on Post-Soul Black Culture*. New York: HarperCollins Publishers, 1992, p. 75.

8. Rose, *Black Noise*, p. 54.

9. Lynn Norment, "Music: Influence of Black Music on White America," *Ebony*, August 1991, p. 42.

10. Quoted in Rose, *Black Noise*, p. 81.

11. Ian Steaman, "Gangsta Rap Runs Risk of Becoming Passé," *Billboard*, September 19, 1992, p. 10.

12. Rose, *Black Noise*, p. 73.

13. Nelson George, *Hip Hop America*. New York: Penguin Books, 1998, pp. 89–90.

14. Gene Santoro, "Public Enemy," *The Nation*, June 25, 1990, p. 90.

15. Quoted in Alan Light, ed., *The Vibe History of Hip Hop*. New York: Three Rivers Press, 1999, pp. 170–71.

16. Quoted in John Leland, "The Moper vs. the Rapper: A Lawsuit, Naturally," *Newsweek*, January 1, 1992, p. 55.

17. Havelock Nelson, "Dissed by Pirates, Dogged by 'Sample Hell,'" *Billboard*, November 28, 1992, p. 123.

18. Johnnie L. Roberts, "The Rap on Rap: It's the Hottest Thing in Music. So Why Won't the Industry Pay More for It?" *Newsweek*, March 1, 1999, p. 45.

Chapter 2: Selling Records or Selling Out?

19. Light, ed., *Vibe History of Hip Hop*, p. 27.

20. Quoted in Light, ed., *Vibe History of Hip Hop*, p. 27.

21. George, *Hip Hop America*, p. 20.

22. Jay Cocks, "U Can't Touch Him; M.C. Hammer Flies High by Making Rap a Pop Sensation," *Time*, August 13, 1990, p. 73.

23. Quoted in Light, ed., *Vibe History of Hip Hop*, p. 128.

24. Quoted in Charles Whitaker, "The Real Story Behind the Rap Revolution," *Ebony*, June 1990, p. 38.

25. Light, ed., *Vibe History of Hip Hop*, p. 29.

26. Quoted in George Moll, "Public Enemy," *Behind the Music*.

27. Quoted in George Moll, "Public Enemy," *Behind the Music*.

28. Hank Shocklee-Sadler, Charles Ridenhour, "Fight the Power," as it appears at www.publicenemy.com/lyrics/lyrics/fight-the-power.php.

29. Quoted in David Samuels, "The Rap on Rap: The 'Black Music' That Isn't Either," *The New Republic*, November 11, 1991, p. 26.

30. George Moll, producer, "Public Enemy," *Behind the Music*, 2000.

31. Steaman, "Gangsta Rap," p. 10.

32. Quoted in Samuels, "The Rap on Rap," p. 29.

33. Jay Cocks, "A Nasty Jolt for the Top Pops: N.W.A.'s Grotesque New Rap Album Soars to No. 1, Raising Questions about Why Ghetto Rage and Brutal Abuse of Women Appeal to Mainstream Listeners," *Time*, July 1, 1991, p. 79.

Chapter 3: Violent Lyrics, Violent Lifestyles

34. *Time*, "Bad Rap: Run-D.M.C. Concert Riot," September 1, 1986, p. 20.

35. "Bad Rap: Run-D.M.C. Concert Riot," p. 20.

36. Tricia Rose, *Black Noise*, p. 134.

37. Michael Marriott, "A Gangster Wake-up Call: Hard-core Stars Are Coming to Hard Ends; Will Their Fans Hear That Message?" *Newsweek*, April 10, 1995, p. 74.

38. *Black Collegian*, "Gangsta Rap: Should It Be Censored?" October 1994, p. 20.

39. Quoted in Havelock Nelson, "Music & Violence: Does Crime Pay? Gangsta Gunplay Sparks Industry Debate," *Billboard*, November 13, 1993, p. 109.

40. Quoted in John Leland, "Gangsta Rap and the Culture of Violence," *Newsweek*, November 29, 1993, p. 64.

41. Quoted in George Moll, "Dr. Dre," *Behind the Music*, 2000.

42. George Will, "America's Slide Into the Sewer: A Confused Society Protects Lungs More Than Minds, Trout More Than Black Women," *Newsweek*, July 30, 1990, p. 64.

43. Quoted in Greg Beets, "Trial Witness Ties Rap to Violent Act," *Billboard*, July 10, 1993, p. 71.

44. Quoted in Beets, "Trial Witness Ties Rap to Violent Act," p. 71.

45. Quoted in Beets, "Trial Witness Ties Rap to Violent Act," p. 71.

46. Quoted in Moll, "Dr. Dre."

47. Quoted in Sally B. Donnelly, "The Fire Around Ice," *Time*, June 22, 1992.

48. Owen Husney, "Hardcore Rappers Are Voice of the Underclass," *Billboard*, June 27, 1992, p. 6.

49. Robin D. G. Kelley, "Straight From Underground: How Rap Music Portrays the Police," *The Nation*, June 8, 1992, p. 793.

50. Husney, "Hardcore Rappers," p. 6.

51. *The Economist*, "Are You Proud of Who You Are?" December 8, 1990, p. 25.

52. Steaman, "Gangsta Rap," p. 10.

53. Quoted in Joy Bennett Kinnon, "Does Rap Have a Future?" *Ebony*, June 1997, p. 76.

54. Steve S. Salem, "Rap Music Mirrors Its Environment," *Billboard*, November 27, 1993, p. 48.

55. Tricia Rose, "Rap Music and the Demonization of Young Black Males," *USA Today* (magazine), May 1994.

56. Marriott, "A Gangster Wake-up Call," p. 74.

57. Johnnie L. Roberts, "Blood on the Record Biz," *Newsweek*, September 23, 1996, p. 69.

58. Quoted in Nelson, "Music & Violence."

59. Quoted in Allison Samuels and David Gates, "Last Tango in Compton: A Founding Father of Gangsta Rap Now Says He's Been There, Done That," *Newsweek*, November 25, 1996.

60. Quoted in Samuels and Gates, "Last Tango in Compton."

Chapter 4: Sexism

61. *The Economist*, "Are You Proud of Who You Are?" p. 25.

62. Quoted in J. R. Reynolds, "Dogg Pound Could Renew Pressure on Time Warner," *Billboard*, July 29, 1995, p. 10.

63. Quoted in Marjorie Rosen, "Rock, Roll and Raunch: Obscenity in Rock and Roll," *People*, July 2, 1990.

64. John Leo, "Polluting Our Popular Culture," *U.S. News & World Report*, July 2, 1990, p. 15.

65. Quoted in *People,* "C. Delores Tucker: Alarmed by What Gangsta Rap Was Doing to African-American Children, She Declared War on a Corporate Media Giant—and Prevailed," December 25, 1995, p. 71.

66. *Black Collegian* "Gangsta Rap: Should It Be Censored?"

67. Murray Forman, "'Movin' Closer to an Independent Funk': Black Feminist Theory, Standpoint, and Women in Rap," *Women's Studies*, January 1994.

68. Quoted in Bill Holland, "House Panel to Examine Rap," *Billboard*, February 19, 1994, p. 1.

69. James D. Johnson, Mike S. Adams, Leslie Ashburn, and William Reed, "Differential Gender Effects of Exposure to Rap Music on African American Adolescents' Acceptance of Teen Dating Violence," *Sex Roles: A Journal of Research,* October 1995.

70. James D. Johnson, Mike S. Adams, Leslie Ashburn, and William Reed, "Differential Gender Effects of Exposure to Rap Music on African American Adolescents' Acceptance of Teen Dating Violence," *Sex Roles: A Journal of Research*, October 1995.

71. Leo, "Polluting Our Popular Culture," p. 15.

72. Henry Louis Gates Jr., "Taking the Rap: Black Intellectuals and the 2 Live Crew Obscenity Case," *The New Republic*, December 3, 1990, p. 4.

73. Rose, *Black Noise*, pp. 15–16.

74. Forman, "'Movin' Closer to an Independent Funk.'"

75. Quoted in Havelock Nelson, "New Female Rappers Play for Keeps," *Billboard*, July 10, 1993.

76. David E. Thigpen, "Not For Men Only: Women Rappers Are Breaking the Mold with a Message of Their Own," *Time*, May 27, 1991, p. 71.

77. Quoted in Light, ed., *Vibe History of Hip Hop*, p. 181.

78. Quoted in Greg Kot, "Lauryn Hill," www.rollingstone.com.

79. Rose, *Black Noise*, p. 154.

80. Quoted in J. R. Reynolds, "Women Rap for Dignity: Defiant Voices Fight Misogyny," *Billboard*, March 26, 1994, p. 13.

81. Quoted in Reynolds, "Women Rap for Dignity."

82. Lucy O'Brien, *She-Bop: The Definitive History of Women in Rock, Pop and Soul.* New York: Penguin Books, 1995, pp. 307–08.

83. Rose, *Black Noise*, p. 150.

84. Forman, "'Movin' Closer to an Independent Funk.'"

85. Nelson, "New Female Rappers Play for Keeps."

Chapter 5: Prejudice

86. Santoro, "Public Enemy."

87. Quoted in Moll, "Public Enemy."

88. Quoted in Santoro, "Public Enemy."

89. Charles Ridenauer, "Welcome to the Terrordome," *Fear of a Black Planet*.

90. Light, ed., *Vibe History of Hip Hop*, p. 172.

91. George, *Hip Hop America*.

92. Quoted in John Leo, "Rap Music's Toxic Fringe Racial Epithets Used by Some Rap Singers," *U.S. News & World Report,* June 29, 1992, p. 19.

93. Quoted in Light, ed., *Vibe History of Hip Hop*, p. 289.

94. Marc Shapiro, *My Rules: The Lauryn Hill Story, An Unauthorized Biography*. New York: Berkley Boulevard Books, 1999, p. 88–89.

95. *Billboard*, "Editorial," November 23, 1991, p. 8.

96.   Mortimer B. Zuckerman, "The Sister Souljah Affair," *U.S. News & World Report*, June 29, 1992, p. 80.

97.   Stephen Rodrick, "Hip Hop Flop: The Failure of Liberal Rap," *The New Republic*, February 8, 1993, p. 18.

98.   Eric Dyson, "Dole's Bad Rap: Senator Bob Dole Criticizes Motion Picture Violence and Gangsta Rap Music," *The Nation,* June 26, 1995.

99.   Quoted in Donnelly, "The Fire Around Ice."

100.   Quoted in Andrew Dansby, "GLAAD Takes Aim at 'Marshall Mathers': Gay Lesbian Alliance Has No Love for Eminem," May 30, 2000, www.rollingstone.com/sections/news/text/newsarticle.asp?afl=&NewsID=10938&LookUp String=6395.

101.   Quoted in Anthony DeCurtis, "Eminem Shouts Back About His Lyrics," July 15, 2000, http://www.rollingstone.com/sections/news/text/newsarticle.asp?afl=&NewsID=11286&LookUp String=6395.

102.   Quoted in Moll, "Public Enemy."

Chapter 6: Rap and Censorship

103.   Quoted in Geoff Boucher, "Tipper's Refrain," www.latimes.com, August 17, 2000.

104.   *Time*, "Making Rap an Issue," March 12, 1990, p. 25.

105.   Quoted in Rosen, "Rock, Roll, and Raunch."

106.   *National Review*, "Underclass Consciousness: Criticism of Rap Group 2 Live Crew," August 20, 1990, p. 14.

107.   Quoted in Rose, *Black Noise*, p. 130.

108.   Quoted in Donnelly, "The Fire Around Ice."

109.   *Billboard*, "Body Count: The Issue Is Censorship," July 18, 1992, p. 4.

110.   Quoted in Light, *Vibe History of Hip Hop*, p. 289.

111.   Quoted in Bill Adler, "Quayle Practices Politics of Distraction," *Billboard*, October 24, 1992.

112.   Quoted in Holland, "House Panel to Examine Rap," p. 1.

Organizations
to Contact

American Civil Liberties Union (ACLU)
132 West 43rd Street
New York, NY 10036
(212) 944-9800
website: www.aclu.org

The ACLU is a group that works to protect the rights and liberties guaranteed U.S. citizens in the Constitution. It opposes the censoring of any form of speech. The ACLU publishes the quarterly newsletter *Civil Liberties Alert* and several handbooks, public policy reports, civil liberties books, and pamphlets, including one on the Freedom of Information Act.

Anti-Defamation League (ADL)
823 United Nations Plaza
New York, NY 10017
(212) 490-2525
website: www.adl.org

An international human rights/civil rights agency, the ADL works through education, legislation, litigation, communication, and persuasion to counteract all forms of anti-Semitism, racism, and intolerance; investigate and expose extremists, bigots, and hate movements; build understanding among racial, religious, and ethnic groups; combat discrimination; and to develop diversity education and training to reduce prejudice. Recently the ADL has taken some rap artists to task for lyrics they believed to be anti-Semitic.

Gay and Lesbian Alliance Against Defamation (GLAAD)
1700 Kalorama Road NW, #101
Washington, DC 20009
(202) 986-0425 • (800) GAY-MEDIA
fax: (202) 986-0470
website: www.glaad.org

GLAAD seeks "to improve the public's attitudes toward homo-sexuality and put an end to violence and discrimination against lesbians and gay men." In recent years GLAAD has criticized some rap musicians for homophobic lyrics.

Parents' Music Resource Center (PMRC)
1500 Arlington Boulevard
Arlington, VA 22209
(703) 527-9466

Founded in 1985, the PMRC works to inform parents about the entertainment industry and, specifically, what is appro-priate for children. The PMRC is the organization that pushed for the parental advisory/explicit lyrics labels for mu-sic that promotes sex, violence, and drug use.

Suggestions for Further Reading

Books

Chuck D and Yusuf Jah, *Fight the Power: Rap, Race, and Reality.* New York: Delacorte Press, 1997. This is the autobiography of Chuck D, the creative force behind Public Enemy. It gives readers insight into his ideology as well as what it was like to be part of a group that broke down quite a few barriers in the world of popular music.

Sach Jenkins, Elliott Wilson, Chairman Mao, Gabriel Alvarez, Theodore Alosius Bawno, Brent Rollins, *Ego Trip's Book of Rap Lists.* New York: Griffin Trade Paperback, 1999. This book is a really entertaining collection of items from the now-defunct rap magazine *Ego Trip*. It contains millions of well-known facts as well as virtually unknown facts compiled in lists—some of which are really funny.

Alan Light, ed., *The Vibe History of Hip Hop.* New York: Three Rivers Press, 1999. This is a great book filled with entertaining essays about rap music. One of the best books found for insight into issues and performers. Its essay format and accessible text make it ideal for young readers who want to learn more about rap music.

Lucy O'Brien, *She-Bop: The Definitive History of Women in Rock, Pop and Soul.* New York: Penguin Books, 1995. O'Brien writes about women in all genres of music, including rap. The book is accessible and highlights many of the issues that women face in the music industry, including sexism.

Alex Ogg et al., *The Hip Hop Years: A History of Rap.* Philadelphia: Trans-Atlantic Publications, Inc., 1999. This is a good resource for the history of rap. It follows hip hop from its beginnings as a New York City block party music up to today's crossover appeal. It also contains some good interviews with some of rap's most important artists and producers.

Ronin Ro, *Have Gun Will Travel: The Spectacular Rise and Violent Fall of Death Row Records*. New York: Doubleday, 1999. Those who are interested in Death Row Records, Suge Knight, and Tupac Shakur will enjoy this book. Ro's writing style is very accessible, but be aware that there is a great deal of profanity in the text.

Marc Shapiro, *My Rules: The Lauryn Hill Story, An Unauthorized Biography*. New York: Berkley Boulevard Books, 1999. This book tells the life story of Lauryn Hill and in so doing informs readers about some of the obstacles women face in the music business.

Internet Sources

lyrics.astraweb.com is an exceptional resource for the lyrics of songs of all genres.

www.mtv.com/news/gallery/ is another great archive of articles about rap music and musicians. It also has live interviews and transcripts of MTV specials such as "When Lyrics Attack," a show they did on lyrics that are prejudiced toward various groups.

www.rollingstone.com is an excellent resource for recent news articles on rap music and some rap artists. The site also has live interviews and video components.

www.thesource.com bills itself as the "largest collection of hip hop information on the Web" and this seems to be true. However, be aware that it is also a chat site and the text is not censored.

www.vibe.com is a good source for current hip hop information. However, there are no archives for past issues available online.

Works Consulted

Books

Nelson George, *Buppies, B-Boys, Baps, & Bohos: Notes on Post-Soul Black Culture.* New York: HarperCollins Publishers, 1992. This book is a compilation of articles and essays written by George. It contains numerous columns, reviews, and essays on rap and its artists.

———, *Hip Hop America.* New York: Penguin Books, 1998. This is a great book on rap music issues and history. George is an entertaining and fairly accessible author who puts many of the most heated debates in rap music in historical and cultural perspective.

Tricia Rose, *Black Noise: Rap Music and Black Culture in Contemporary America.* Hanover, NH: Wesleyan University Press, 1994. This is one of the finest books available on issues in rap music. Too complex for young adult readers, it is however an excellent background resource.

Periodicals and Internet Sources

Bill Adler, "Quayle Practices Politics of Distraction," *Billboard,* October 24, 1992.

Greg Beets, "Trial Witness Ties Rap to Violent Act," *Billboard,* July 10, 1993.

Billboard, "Editorial," November 23, 1991.

Billboard, "Body Count: The Issue is Censorship," July 18, 1992.

Geoff Boucher, "Tipper's Refrain," www.latimes.com, August 17, 2000.

Jay Cocks, "A Nasty Jolt for the Top Pops: N.W.A.'s Grotesque New Rap Album Soars to No. 1, Raising Questions about Why Ghetto Rage and Brutal Abuse of Women Appeal to Mainstream Listeners," *Time*, July 1, 1991.

———, "U Can't Touch Him; M.C. Hammer Flies High by Making Rap a Pop Sensation," *Time*, August 13, 1990.

Andrew Dansby, "GLAAD Takes Aim at 'Marshall Mathers': Gay Lesbian Alliance Has No Love for Eminem," May 30, 2000, www.rollingstone.com/sections/news/text/newsarticle.asp?afl=&NewsID=10938&LookUpString=6395.

Anthony DeCurtis, "Eminem Shouts Back About His Lyrics," July 15, 2000, www.rollingstone.com/sections/news/text/news article.asp?afl=&NewsID=11286&LookUpString=6395.

Sally B. Donnelly, "The Fire Around Ice," *Time*, June 22, 1992.

Eric Dyson, "Dole's Bad Rap: Senator Bob Dole Criticizes Motion Picture Violence and Gangsta Rap Music," *The Nation*, June 26, 1995.

The Economist, "Are You Proud of Who You Are?" December 8, 1990.

Murray Forman, "'Movin' Closer to an Independent Funk': Black Feminist Theory, Standpoint, and Women in Rap," *Women's Studies*, January 1994.

"Gangsta Rap: Should It Be Censored?" *Black Collegian*, October 1994.

David Gates with Peter Katel, "The Importance of Being Nasty," *Newsweek*, July 2, 1990.

Henry Louis Gates Jr., "Taking the Rap: Black Intellectuals and the 2 Live Crew Obscenity Case," *The New Republic*, December 3, 1990.

Christopher Hitchens, "Minority Report," *The Nation*, July 30–August 6, 1990.

Bill Holland, "Anti-Rap Campaign to be Directed at 5 Major Record Labels," *Billboard*, June 8, 1996.

———, "House Panel to Examine Rap," *Billboard*, February 19, 1994.

Owen Husney, "Hardcore Rappers Are Voice of the Underclass," *Billboard*, June 27, 1992.

O'Shea Jackson, "Black Korea," *Death Certificate*.

James D. Johnson, Mike S. Adams, Leslie Ashburn, and William Reed, "Differential Gender Effects of Exposure to Rap Music on African American Adolescents' Acceptance of Teen Dating Violence," *Sex Roles: A Journal of Research,* October 1995.

Robin D.G. Kelley, "Straight From Underground: How Rap Music Portrays the Police," *The Nation*, June 8, 1992.

Joy Bennett Kinnon, "Does Rap Have a Future?" *Ebony*, June 1997.

Greg Kot, "Lauryn Hill," www.rollingstone.com.

John Leland, "Gangsta Rap and the Culture of Violence," *Newsweek,* November 29, 1993.

———, "The Moper vs. the Rapper: A Lawsuit, Naturally," *Newsweek*, January 1, 1992.

John Leo, "Polluting Our Popular Culture," *U.S. News & World Report*, July 2, 1990.

———, "Rap Music's Toxic Fringe: Racial Epithets Used by Some Rap Singers," *U.S. News & World Report*, June 29, 1992.

Michael Marriott, "A Gangster Wake-up Call: Hard-core Stars Are Coming to Hard Ends; Will Their Fans Hear That Message?" *Newsweek*, April 10, 1995.

Rhoda E. McKinney, "What's Behind the Rise of Rap?" *Ebony*, January 1989.

George Moll, "Public Enemy," *Behind the Music*, 2000.

———, "Dr. Dre," *Behind the Music*, 2000.

National Review, "Underclass Consciousness: Criticism of Rap Group 2 Live Crew," August 20, 1990.

Havelock Nelson, "Dissed by Pirates, Dogged by 'Sample Hell,'" *Billboard,* November 28, 1992.

———, "Music & Violence: Does Crime Pay? Gangsta Gunplay Sparks Industry Debate," *Billboard*, November 13, 1993.

———, "New Female Rappers Play for Keeps," *Billboard*, July 10, 1993.

Lynn Norment, "Music: Influence of Black Music on White America," *Ebony*, August 1991.

People, "C. Delores Tucker: Alarmed by What Gangsta Rap Was Doing to African-American Children, She Declared War on a Corporate Media Giant—and Prevailed," December 25, 1995.

J. R. Reynolds, "Dogg Pound Could Renew Pressure on Time Warner," *Billboard*, July 29, 1995.

———, "Women Rap for Dignity: Defiant Voices Fight Misogyny," *Billboard*, March 26, 1994.

Charles Ridenauer, "Welcome to the Terrordome," *Fear of a Black Planet.*

Johnnie L. Roberts, "Blood on the Record Biz," *Newsweek*, September 23, 1996.

———, "The Rap on Rap: It's the Hottest Thing in Music. So Why Won't the Industry Pay More for It?" *Newsweek*, March 1, 1999.

Stephen Rodrick, "Hip Hop Flop: The Failure of Liberal Rap," *The New Republic*, February 8, 1993.

Tricia Rose, "Rap Music and the Demonization of Young Black Males," *USA Today* (magazine), May 1994.

Marjorie Rosen, "Rock, Roll and Raunch: Obscenity in Rock and Roll," *People*, July 2, 1990.

Steve S. Salem, "Rap Music Mirrors Its Environment," *Billboard*, November 27, 1993.

Allison Samuels and David Gates, "Last Tango in Compton: A Founding Father of Gangsta Rap Now Says He's Been There, Done That," *Newsweek*, November 25, 1996.

David Samuels, "The Rap on Rap: The 'Black Music' That Isn't Either," *The New Republic*, November 11, 1991.

Gene Santoro, "Public Enemy," *The Nation*, June 25, 1990.

Hank Shocklee-Sadler, Charles Ridenhour, "Fight the Power," as it appears at www.public-enemy.com/lyrics/lyrics/fight-the-power.php.

Ian Steaman, "Gangsta Rap Runs Risk of Becoming Passé," *Billboard*, September 19, 1992.

David E. Thigpen, "Not For Men Only: Women Rappers Are Breaking the Mold with a Message of Their Own," *Time,* May 27, 1991.

Time, "Bad Rap: Run-D.M.C. Concert Riot," September 1, 1986.

Time, "Making Rap an Issue," March 12, 1990.

Charles Whitaker, "The Real Story Behind the Rap Revolution," *Ebony,* June 1990.

George Will, "America's Slide Into the Sewer: A Confused Society Protects Lungs More Than Minds, Trout More Than Black Women," *Newsweek*, July 30, 1990.

Mortimer B. Zuckerman, "The Sister Souljah Affair," *U.S. News & World Report*, June 29, 1992.

Index

Picture Credits

Cover Photo: © Fotex/B. Kuhmstedt/Shooting Star
Archive Photos, 70
Associated Press, 44, 59, 69, 72, 74, 80, 90
Associated Press/Columbia Pictures, 55
© Bettmann/Corbis, 38, 43, 49
© Corbis, 40
Fotos International/Archive Photos, 32, 51
The Gamma Liaison Network, 47
© Lynn Goldsmith/Corbis, 21, 30
© Susan Greenwood/The Gamma Liaison Network, 7
© Robbie Jack/Corbis, 57
© Barry King/The Gamma Liaison Network, 46
© Krasmer/Trebitz/The Gamma Liaison Network, 85
Library of Congress, 91
© John Marshall Mantel/Corbis, 15
Frank Micelotta/Newscom.com, 17
Photodisc, 33, 45
© Peter Poby/Corbis, 10
© Neal Preston/Corbis, 27
Reuters/Ethan Miller/Archive Photos, 52
Reuters/Fred Prouser/Archive Photos, 57, 64
Reuters/Jeff Christensen/Archive Photos, 61, 77
Reuters/Lee Celano/Archive Photos, 88
Reuters/Lou Dematteis/Archive Photos, 86
Reuters/Mike Segar/Archive Photos, 41
© Reuters NewMedia Inc./Corbis, 19
SAGA/Evan Yee/Archive Photos, 82
© S.I.N./Corbis, 12, 13, 26, 28, 37, 67
Jason Trigg/Archive Photos, 62

About the Author

Jennifer Keeley is a freelance writer who lives and works in Seattle, Washington. She graduated from Carleton College in 1996 with a degree in history and her teaching certificate. She has taught history and social studies in both the Seattle and Minneapolis Public Schools.